Table of Contents

Introduction: The definition and scope of African fusion cocktails 4

- The history and culture of African drinks and spirits 5

- The main themes and objectives of the book 7

Chapter 1: Baobab - The Origin and Distribution of Baobab in Africa 9

- The uses and benefits of baobab fruit and powder in Africa 11

- The examples and recipes of cocktails using baobab in Africa 13

Chapter 2: Marula- The Origin and Distribution of Marula in Africa 15

- The uses and benefits of marula fruit and liqueur in Africa 17

- The examples and recipes of cocktails using marula in Africa 18

Chapter 3: Tamarind - The Origin and Distribution of Tamarind in Africa 21

- The uses and benefits of tamarind pulp and juice in Africa 23

- The examples and recipes of cocktails using tamarind in Africa 24

Chapter 4: Hibiscus- The Origin and Distribution of Hibiscus in Africa 27

- The uses and benefits of hibiscus flowers and tea in Africa 29

- The examples and recipes of cocktails using hibiscus in Africa 30

Chapter 5: Ginger - The Origin and Distribution of Ginger in Africa 34

- The uses and benefits of ginger root and beer in Africa 36

- The examples and recipes of cocktails using ginger in Africa 38

Chapter 6: Rooibos - The Origin and Distribution of Rooibos in South Africa 41

- The uses and benefits of rooibos leaves and tea in South Africa 43

- The examples and recipes of cocktails using rooibos in South Africa 45

Chapter 7: Coffee - The Origin and Distribution of Coffee in Africa 47

- The uses and benefits of coffee beans and brew in Africa 49

- The examples and recipes of cocktails using coffee in Africa 51

Chapter 8: Cocoa - The Origin and Distribution of Cocoa in Africa 53

- The uses and benefits of cocoa beans and chocolate in Africa 55

- The examples and recipes of cocktails using cocoa in Africa 57

Chapter 9: Mint - The Origin and Distribution of Mint in Africa 60

- The uses and benefits of mint leaves and oil in Africa..62
- The examples and recipes of cocktails using mint in Africa 64
Chapter 10: Cardamom - The Origin and Distribution of Cardamom in Africa 66
- The uses and benefits of cardamom pods and seeds in Africa 68
- The examples and recipes of cocktails using cardamom in Africa 70
Chapter 11: Cinnamon - The Origin and Distribution of Cinnamon in Africa 72
- The uses and benefits of cinnamon bark and powder in Africa..74
- The examples and recipes of cocktails using cinnamon in Africa 76
Chapter 12: Nutmeg - The Origin and Distribution of Nutmeg in Africa 78
- The uses and benefits of nutmeg seeds and powder in Africa 80
- The examples and recipes of cocktails using nutmeg in Africa..82
Chapter 13: Clove – The origin and distribution of clove in Africa 85
- The uses and benefits of clove buds and oil in Africa..87
- The examples and recipes of cocktails using clove in Africa 89
Chapter 14: Vanilla- The Origin and Distribution of Vanilla in Africa................................92
- The uses and benefits of vanilla beans and extract in Africa 94
- The examples and recipes of cocktails using vanilla in Africa 96
Chapter 15: Saffron - The Origin and Distribution of Saffron in Africa..............................99
- The uses and benefits of saffron threads and powder in Africa 101
- The examples and recipes of cocktails using saffron in Africa..................................... 103
Chapter 16: Palm Wine - The Origin and Distribution of Palm Wine in Africa 106
- The production and consumption of palm wine in Africa 108
- The examples and recipes of cocktails using palm wine in Africa 110
Chapter 17: Sorghum Beer - The Origin and Distribution of Sorghum Beer in Africa 112
- The production and consumption of sorghum beer in Africa...................................... 114
- The examples and recipes of cocktails using sorghum beer in Africa.......................... 116
Chapter 18: Honey Wine- The Origin and Distribution of Honey Wine in Africa 119
- The production and consumption of honey wine in Africa.. 121
- The examples and recipes of cocktails using honey wine in Africa 123
Chapter 19: Amarula Cream: The Origin and Distribution of Amarula Cream in South Africa
.... 126
- The production and consumption of amarula cream in South Africa 128
- The examples and recipes of cocktails using amarula cream in South Africa 130

Chapter 20: Future and Innovation - The Current Trends and Issues of African Fusion Cocktails 133

- The prospects and challenges of African fusion cocktails 135

- The role of African fusion cocktails in the vision and action of African futures 137

Conclusion- The summary and synthesis of the main findings and arguments of the book 140

- The implications and contributions of the book to the field of food studies and African studies 141

- The suggestions and recommendations for further research and exploration on African fusion cocktails 144

Introduction: The definition and scope of African fusion cocktails

African fusion cocktails are creating a stir in the beverage industry, offering a unique blend of traditional African flavors with modern mixology techniques. This emerging trend has gained popularity in recent years, as it provides an exciting fusion of cultures and tastes that intrigue and delight cocktail enthusiasts.

The definition of African fusion cocktails is the blending of traditional African ingredients, flavors, and spirits with international mixology techniques. It involves taking traditional African drinks, such as palm wine, sorghum beer, or marula fruit liqueur, and incorporating them into a contemporary cocktail menu. African fusion cocktails aim to showcase the diverse flavors found across the continent, highlighting the richness of African culture through its distinctive beverages.

The scope of African fusion cocktails is vast, as Africa is a continent with a wide range of culinary traditions and ingredients. Each region has its own unique offerings, from the hearty and spiced flavors of North Africa to the tropically infused beverages of West Africa. The fusion of these flavors with modern cocktail-making methods allows for a captivating and adventurous drinking experience.

One popular example of an African fusion cocktail is the "Safari Sunset." This cocktail combines the tangy flavors of marula fruit liqueur, which is derived from the native African marula tree, with vodka, orange juice, and a splash of grenadine. The result is a refreshing and visually stunning drink that captures the essence of an African sunset.

Another intriguing option is the "Savannah Spice." This cocktail incorporates the bold flavors of African spices, such as ginger and clove, with rum, lime juice, and a touch of honey. The combination of heat from the spices and the sweetness from the honey creates a tantalizing and aromatic beverage that transports drinkers to the heart of Africa.

The cocktail scene in Africa is booming, with mixologists and bartenders embracing the wealth of natural ingredients available to create innovative and memorable drinks. From traditional drinks like South Africa's Rooibos Old Fashioned, made with the country's renowned rooibos tea, to Sudan's Sinikip Beet Margarita, utilizing fresh beets, the possibilities are endless.

African fusion cocktails not only offer a new and exciting drinking experience but also provide an opportunity to promote local African products and stimulate economic growth. By incorporating traditional African ingredients into cocktails, these creations not only showcase the rich tapestry of African culture but also support local farms and producers.

In conclusion, African fusion cocktails are a delightful blend of traditional African ingredients with contemporary mixology techniques. They showcase the diverse flavors and culinary heritage of the continent, offering a unique and memorable drinking experience. As the popularity of this trend continues to grow, we can anticipate more exciting African-inspired concoctions that truly capture the essence of the continent.

- The history and culture of African drinks and spirits

The history and culture of African drinks and spirits is a fascinating tapestry that spans thousands of years and encompasses a wide variety of beverages. From ancient brewing techniques to traditional rituals surrounding the consumption of alcoholic beverages, Africa has a rich and vibrant drinking culture that reflects the diversity of its people and their traditions.

One of the oldest known alcoholic beverages in Africa is mead, a honey-based fermented drink that has been enjoyed for centuries. This ancient libation can be traced back to ancient Egypt, where it was consumed by pharaohs and nobles. Mead has a long association with celebration and ritual, and it is often used in ceremonies and festivities throughout the continent.

In West Africa, palm wine holds a special place in the hearts and palates of many people. Made from the sap of various palm trees, this traditional drink is loved for its sweet and tangy flavor. Palm wine has been produced and consumed in the region for centuries, with the process of extracting the sap requiring great skill and expertise.

Moving eastward, Ethiopia is renowned for its coffee culture. The country is often referred to as the birthplace of coffee, with legends dating back to the 9th century, which speak of a goatherd discovering the stimulating properties of coffee beans. Today, Ethiopian coffee is loved worldwide for its unique flavors and diverse aromas. In Ethiopia, coffee ceremonies are a significant social event, symbolizing friendship and hospitality. The beans are roasted, ground, and brewed in front of guests, with elaborate rituals and traditions surrounding the process.

Central and southern Africa offer a range of unique beverages as well. Savannah cider, traditionally brewed and enjoyed in Zimbabwe, is an alcoholic beverage made from fermented marula fruit. This wild fruit has been a staple of the region for generations, and the cider is known for its rich fruity taste and mild alcoholic content. Fermented maize beverages, such as the iconic South African drink called umqombothi or African beer, are also popular in these regions. Made from mielie meal (a corn-based porridge) and traditionally brewed by women, umqombothi plays a vital role in social gatherings and celebrations.

In addition to these traditional drinks, modern African spirits and liqueurs are also making their mark on the global stage. Amarula, a creamy liqueur made from marula fruit, is one such example. Originating from South Africa, Amarula has gained international recognition and is enjoyed as a standalone drink or as an ingredient in various cocktails.

The history and culture of African drinks and spirits continue to evolve with the changing times, yet their deep-rooted connection to traditions and ancient practices remains strong. As African nations embrace their cultural heritage and introduce their unique beverages to the world, the rich tapestry of African drinking culture adds depth, flavor, and traditions to the global beverage industry.

- The main themes and objectives of the book

In the book, the author explores a myriad of themes and objectives, elevating the narrative and adding depth to the story. Here are some of the main themes and objectives underlying the book:

1. Identity and Self-Discovery: One of the central themes of the book revolves around the characters' journeys in discovering their true identities. Through introspection, external influences, and pivotal life experiences, the characters explore and redefine their sense of self, causing a profound transformation.

2. Love and Relationships: Love serves as both a theme and objective of the book. The author delves deep into the complexities of human relationships, exploring various types of love- romantic, familial, and platonic. The characters navigate their love lives, facing challenges, heartbreak, and ultimately finding personal fulfillment and growth through these connections.

3. Redemption and Forgiveness: Another significant theme in the book is the pursuit of redemption and the power of forgiveness. The author impressively portrays the characters' struggle for redemption, illustrating their path towards self-forgiveness and acceptance. Through this exploration, the book sheds light on the profound healing and growth that can result from a compassionate and forgiving mindset.

4. Societal and Cultural Norms: The book also aims to critically examine and challenge societal and cultural norms. Whether it is gender roles, societal expectations, or societal pressures, the author emphasizes the importance of self-liberation and questioning these norms to live an authentic life. The book encourages readers to challenge the status quo for personal and collective advancement.

5. Overcoming Adversity: The book explores the resilience of the human spirit and the capacity to overcome adversities. Through various challenges and obstacles faced by the characters, the author portrays their determination and perseverance to rise above their circumstances. This theme highlights the significance of hope, courage, and personal growth in navigating life's hardships.

6. Moral Dilemmas and Ethical Choices: The author also grapples with complex moral dilemmas and ethical choices faced by the characters. The book prompts readers to reflect upon the consequences of their actions and the blurred lines between right and wrong. It delves into the complexity of decision-making and explores how choices can shape one's personal journey and impact others.

Overall, the book skillfully weaves together these themes and objectives to craft a thought-provoking and compelling narrative. As readers delve into the intricacies of the characters' experiences, they are immersed in a world where personal growth, human connection, forgiveness, and self-discovery are at the heart of the story.

Chapter 1: Baobab - The Origin and Distribution of Baobab in Africa

The baobab tree, scientifically known as Adansonia, is a fascinating and iconic species that has captivated the curiosity of people throughout history. With its massive trunks and distinctive bottle-shaped form, the baobab tree holds a significant place in African culture, traditions, and ecosystems. In this chapter, we will delve into the origin and distribution of the baobab tree in Africa, exploring its historical significance and ecological importance.

1.1 Ancient Origins
The baobab tree is believed to be one of the oldest living trees on the planet, with fossil evidence indicating its existence approximately 70 million years ago. This means that these iconic giants have witnessed the rise and fall of different civilizations throughout history. Baobabs have stood the test of time, adapting and surviving in various environments across the African continent.

1.2 African Distribution
The baobab tree is native to Africa, specifically to the mainland and different islands off its coast. It is widely distributed from the north, covering areas like Senegal, through Central Africa, and down to South Africa. Baobabs are sparsely scattered across diverse ecosystems, occupying a wide range of habitats, from arid savannahs to lush tropical forests.

1.2.1 West Africa
In West Africa, baobabs are a common sight and cultural icon. Nations like Senegal, Mali, Burkina Faso, Ivory Coast, and Ghana host a significant number of these majestic trees. They flourish in the dry savannah regions, where their presence dominates the landscapes, often painted against the backdrop of beautiful sunsets.

1.2.2 East Africa

Moving to East Africa, countries like Tanzania, Kenya, and Madagascar showcase an enchanting diversity of baobab species. The islands off the coast, particularly Madagascar, are home to some of the most unique and endemic baobab varieties. The baobab forests in these regions are not only of ecological importance, but they also hold cultural and economic value for local communities.

1.2.3 South Africa

In South Africa, baobabs are found in the northern provinces and exhibit a notable adaptation to the arid climates of these areas. They stand tall in the dry landscapes, providing water sources, shelter, and sustenance for a variety of plant and animal species. Baobabs play a vital role in maintaining the ecosystems of the region by providing habitats and acting as ecological sentinels.

1.3 Cultural Significance

The baobab tree is deeply interwoven with African culture and traditions. It is often referred to as the "Tree of Life" due to its numerous uses and tremendous resilience. African communities have revered this tree for centuries and integrated it into their daily lives. From its fruits, leaves, and bark to its hollow trunks used for shelter and storage, baobabs have provided sustenance, medicine, and materials for traditional practices.

1.4 Ecological Importance

Beyond its cultural significance, the baobab tree plays a crucial role in African ecosystems. Its massive trunks act as reservoirs, storing vast amounts of water during the rainy season to be used during drought periods. This feature allows other plants and animals to survive in arid environments. Baobabs also provide essential habitats for various birds, mammals, insects, and even epiphytic plants, further contributing to biodiversity conservation.

In conclusion, the baobab tree has emerged as a symbol of African landscapes and its people. With its origins dating back millions of years, this iconic species has withstood the test of time across diverse environments in Africa. The significance of the baobab tree goes well beyond its stunning physical appearance, as it holds a vital place in African culture, traditions, and ecosystems. Understanding the origin and distribution of baobabs is crucial for appreciating their historical and ecological importance throughout the African continent.

- The uses and benefits of baobab fruit and powder in Africa

The baobab tree (Adansonia) is native to Africa and has been revered for centuries by the indigenous people of the continent. Besides providing shade and shelter, the baobab tree yields a highly nutritious fruit known as baobab fruit or "superfruit." In recent years, the uses and benefits of baobab fruit and powder have gained significant attention worldwide.

1. Nutritional powerhouse:
Baobab fruit is packed with essential nutrients, making it a nutritional powerhouse. It is exceptionally rich in vitamin C, containing six times more vitamin C than oranges. Additionally, it is a rich source of minerals such as potassium, calcium, and magnesium. The fruit pulp also contains beneficial dietary fiber and antioxidants, which contribute to its various health benefits.

2. Boosts immunity:
The high vitamin C content found in baobab fruit helps boost the immune system, fortifying the body's natural defenses against illness and infection. Regular consumption of baobab fruit-based products can help reduce the risk of common ailments like cold and flu.

3. Improves digestive health:
Baobab fruit is abundant in dietary fiber, which aids in maintaining a healthy digestive system. Fiber is known to support regular bowel movements, prevent constipation, and promote the growth of gut-friendly bacteria. Baobab fruit has even been used traditionally to alleviate symptoms of diarrhea and other gastrointestinal issues.

4. Supports radiant skin:
Baobab fruit powder contains antioxidants that help fight free radicals, harmful substances known to cause skin damage and premature aging. The high vitamin C content also plays a crucial role in skin health, boosting collagen production, and enhancing the skin's elasticity and vitality. Additionally, baobab's moisturizing properties make it a popular ingredient in skincare products.

5. Energy booster:
The natural sugars in baobab fruit, combined with its high vitamin C content, make it an excellent natural energy booster. Baobab fruit provides a slow-release energy source, preventing blood sugar spikes and regulating energy levels throughout the day.

6. Helps control blood sugar levels:
While baobab fruit contains natural sugars, research suggests that it can help stabilize blood sugar levels. The fiber content of baobab slows down the release of sugars into the bloodstream, preventing rapid spikes and supporting healthy blood sugar management.

7. Weight management:
Due to its high fiber content, baobab fruit can aid in weight management by promoting a feeling of fullness and reducing excessive snacking. Regularly incorporating baobab fruit or powder into your diet can help control cravings and support healthy weight loss.

8. Sustainable livelihoods:
The increasing demand for baobab fruit and powder worldwide offers significant economic opportunities for communities in Africa. By harnessing the potential of baobab products, local farmers and communities can create sustainable livelihoods, generating income and improving their quality of life.

In conclusion, the uses and benefits of baobab fruit and powder are plentiful, providing a natural and nutritious resource for people across Africa and beyond. From its ability to support immunity, nourish the skin, and aid in digestion to its potential in promoting sustainable livelihoods, baobab fruit and powder truly exemplify the power of traditional African knowledge and innovation.

- The examples and recipes of cocktails using baobab in Africa

Africa is well-known for its rich cultural heritage, diverse landscapes, and unique ingredients. One such ingredient that holds immense significance in African cuisine and mixology is the baobab fruit. Known as the "Tree of Life" due to its various uses, the baobab fruit has been utilized in traditional African recipes for centuries, including the art of mixing cocktails. In this article, we will explore the delicious examples and recipes of cocktails using baobab in Africa.

1. Baobab Margarita:
This refreshing twist on a classic Margarita combines the tangy flavors of baobab fruit with the zing of lime and the kick of tequila. To make this cocktail, start by mixing freshly squeezed lime juice, agave syrup, baobab fruit powder, and silver tequila in a shaker. Shake vigorously and strain the mixture into a salt-rimmed glass filled with ice cubes. Garnish with a slice of lime and enjoy the tropical flavors of Africa.

2. Baobab Mojito:
A traditional Mojito infused with baobab adds a unique twist to this beloved cocktail. Start by muddling fresh mint leaves with baobab fruit powder and brown sugar in a glass. Add lime juice and white rum, and give it a good stir. Fill the glass with crushed ice and top it up with soda water. Garnish with a sprig of mint and a slice of lime. Sip on this baobab-infused Mojito to experience a taste of Africa.

3. Baobab Sunrise:
Bring the colors of the African sunrise to your cocktail glass with this vibrant creation. Begin by mixing baobab fruit powder with freshly squeezed orange

juice until well combined. Fill a tall glass with ice cubes and pour in the baobab-orange mixture. Slowly pour grenadine syrup down the side of the glass to create the sunrise effect. Stir gently and garnish with a slice of orange. Savor the visual delight and tropical fruity flavors of this baobab cocktail.

4. Baobab Martini:
Stir up a sophisticated baobab Martini to celebrate the flavors of Africa in style. This cocktail combines the richness of baobab fruit powder with the smoothness of vodka. To make this cocktail, pour vodka, baobab fruit powder, and simple syrup into a mixing glass filled with ice. Stir vigorously until chilled, then strain the mixture into a chilled Martini glass. Garnish with a twist of lemon peel or a sprig of rosemary for added elegance. Sip on this exotic Martini and indulge in the essence of Africa.

5. Baobab Rum Punch:
Transport yourself to the tropical beaches of Africa with this luscious baobab-infused Rum Punch. In a jug, mix baobab fruit powder, freshly squeezed pineapple juice, rum, and a splash of grenadine syrup. Stir well and refrigerate for an hour to allow the flavors to meld together. Serve in tall glasses filled with ice and garnish with pineapple wedges and a maraschino cherry. Sip on this tantalizing Rum Punch and feel the warmth of the African sun.

These are just a few examples of the countless cocktails that can be created using baobab in Africa. The baobab fruit's tangy and tropical flavors blend seamlessly with other ingredients, offering a unique twist to classic cocktails. So, shake, stir, and savor the taste of Africa by incorporating baobab into your future mixology adventures.

Chapter 2: Marula- The Origin and Distribution of Marula in Africa

Marula (Sclerocarya birrea) is a fascinating and valuable tree found across Africa. Its origins can be traced back thousands of years, making it an important part of the continent's cultural and ecological history. In this chapter, we will delve into the origin and distribution of marula, exploring its journey through time and its current presence throughout Africa.

Origin of Marula:
The marula tree is endemic to sub-Saharan Africa, with fossil evidence suggesting that it has been present on the continent for over 10,000 years. The exact origins of marula are still debated among researchers, but it is widely believed to have originated in the miombo woodlands of southern Africa, specifically in what is now Zimbabwe, Botswana, and South Africa.

Distribution of Marula:
Over time, marula has spread across Africa due to its ability to adapt to diverse climatic conditions. Today, marula can be found throughout various countries in the southern, eastern, and western parts of the continent. Its distribution extends from Mozambique, to Zimbabwe, Kenya, Tanzania, Zambia, Angola, Namibia, Botswana, and South Africa, encompassing a wide range of ecosystems, from grasslands to woodlands.

Ecological Factors Influencing Distribution:
Several ecological factors influence the distribution of marula in Africa. While in general, it thrives in regions with a temperate climate and mild winters, it can tolerate variations in temperature and precipitation. The tree prefers well-drained sandy or loamy soils, thereby often found in areas with these soil characteristics. Additionally, marula trees require a certain amount of sunlight for growth, so they are commonly found in open savannahs or woodland gaps.

Importance in African Culture:
Marula has an indispensable role in African culture and everyday life. The tree holds deep cultural significance for many indigenous communities, who recognize its value for food, medicine, and other practical uses. Marula fruits have long been harvested and eaten, providing essential nutrition during times of scarcity. In addition, its bark, leaves, and roots are used in traditional medicinal practices, treating ailments ranging from stomach ailments to toothache. Marula also plays a part in spiritual rituals, traditionally symbolizing fertility and abundance. For some communities, it holds a sacred status, and its fruit is shared during communal gatherings and ceremonies.

Commercial Value and Sustainable Harvesting:
In recent years, the economic value of marula has gained recognition beyond traditional uses. The tree's fruit, known for its juicy and tangy flavor, has been used to produce marula-based beverages, such as juices, jams, liqueurs, and even beers. The extraction of marula oil has increased in popularity due to its cosmetic and medicinal properties. However, it is crucial to prioritize sustainable harvesting practices to ensure the conservation and longevity of marula trees. Efforts such as community-based management systems and the establishment of fair trade agreements have been implemented to safeguard the tree's sustainability and the livelihoods of local communities.

Marula's origin and distribution reflect its enduring presence in Africa's landscape and culture. From its ancient beginnings in the miombo woodlands to its current distribution in diverse ecosystems across the continent, the marula tree has profoundly impacted the livelihoods of communities and contributed to the ecological richness of Africa. Preserving its cultural significance and ecological importance while ensuring sustainable utilization will be key factors in securing the future of this remarkable tree.

- The uses and benefits of marula fruit and liqueur in Africa

Marula fruit and liqueur have been integral parts of African culture and traditions for centuries. Native to the southern regions of Africa, this fruit, derived from the marula tree (Sclerocarya birrea), holds numerous uses and benefits, ranging from its nutritional value to its economic importance.

The marula fruit is often hailed as a nutritional powerhouse. It is rich in Vitamin C, packed with antioxidants, and contains high levels of essential minerals such as potassium, iron, and magnesium. Vitamin C contributes to the immune system's proper functioning and helps collagen production in the body, leading to healthier bones, skin, and blood vessels. The antioxidants found in marula fruit play a vital role in neutralizing harmful free radicals in the body, reducing the risk of chronic diseases such as cancer and heart ailments.

Traditionally, marula fruit has also been used for its medicinal properties. Its bark, leaves, fruits, and nuts have been employed in African traditional medicines to treat various ailments. The bark is often used to alleviate fever and stomach ailments, while the leaves have been recognized for their anti-inflammatory properties. Additionally, marula oil, extracted from the fruit's nuts, is celebrated for its moisturizing, anti-aging, and healing properties, making it a sought-after ingredient in cosmetics and skincare products worldwide.

Beyond its health benefits, marula fruit has significant cultural and economic importance in many African societies. It holds a place of honor during festive occasions and traditional ceremonies, symbolizing fertility and abundance. The marula fruit harvest often marks a joyous occasion, bringing communities together to celebrate and share the bountiful harvest. It is during these times that marula fruit is also used to produce a popular African alcoholic beverage, marula liqueur.

The process of making marula liqueur involves fermenting the ripe marula fruit, capturing its unique flavors to create a truly African spirit. The liqueur is known for its smooth, sweet taste, often compared to a fruity caramel blend. In many African countries, such as South Africa, Botswana, and Zimbabwe, marula liqueur holds cultural significance as a symbol of community, unity, and celebration.

Moreover, marula liqueur has progressively gained popularity in international markets for its distinctive taste and aromatic qualities. It has become an exciting addition to cocktail recipes, offering a tropical and exotic twist to classic drinks. In recent years, marula liqueur production has provided significant economic opportunities for local communities, fostering entrepreneurship, job creation, and contributing to sustainable development in rural areas of Africa.

In conclusion, the marula fruit and liqueur hold multifaceted uses and benefits in Africa. From their nutritional value to their cultural and economic importance, they play an integral role in African cuisine, traditions, and economies. Whether enjoyed fresh, used in traditional medicine, or fermented into a tantalizing liqueur, marula fruit continues to captivate both the local population and the wider world with its rich history, flavors, and potential.

- The examples and recipes of cocktails using marula in Africa

Africa is a continent known for its diverse and unique flavors. And when it comes to cocktails, one ingredient that stands out is marula. Marula is a fruit that grows on the marula tree, found in various regions of Africa. It has been used for centuries by local communities as a source of food and traditional medicine. In recent times, it has also gained popularity as a key ingredient in cocktails, thanks to its distinct flavor and rich history.

Marula is often referred to as the "African fruit of miracles" because of the many uses and benefits it offers. From its sweet and tangy taste to its high vitamin C content, this fruit quickly became a favorite among mixologists looking to create unique and refreshing cocktails.

Here are a few examples of cocktails that incorporate marula for a taste of Africa:

1. Marula Martini:
Ingredients:
- 1.5 oz marula liqueur
- 1 oz vodka
- 0.5 oz simple syrup
- Juice from half a lime
- Ice cubes

Instructions:
1. Place a few ice cubes in a cocktail shaker.
2. Add the marula liqueur, vodka, simple syrup, and lime juice.
3. Shake vigorously for about 30 seconds.
4. Strain the mixture into a chilled martini glass.
5. Garnish with a lime twist or a marula fruit slice.
6. Serve and enjoy!

2. Marula Mojito:
Ingredients:
- 1.5 oz marula liqueur
- 4-6 fresh mint leaves
- 0.5 oz lime juice
- 1 tbsp white sugar
- Soda water
- Ice cubes

Instructions:
1. In a tall glass, muddle the mint leaves, lime juice, and sugar together until the mint releases its aroma.
2. Fill the glass with ice cubes.

3. Pour the marula liqueur over the ice.
4. Top it off with soda water and stir gently.
5. Garnish with a sprig of fresh mint and a lime wedge.
6. Serve and enjoy!

3. Marula Sunrise:
Ingredients:
- 1.5 oz marula liqueur
- 3 oz orange juice
- 0.5 oz grenadine syrup
- Ice cubes

Instructions:
1. Fill a highball glass with ice cubes.
2. Pour the marula liqueur over the ice.
3. Add the orange juice, leaving some space at the top for the grenadine.
4. Slowly pour the grenadine syrup into the glass, allowing it to sink to the bottom.
5. Do not stir the mixture to maintain the distinct layers.
6. Garnish with an orange slice or a marula fruit wedge.
7. Serve with a straw and enjoy!

These are just a few examples of the many ways marula can be incorporated into cocktails, bringing an authentic taste of Africa to your palate. So next time you want to experiment with your drink choices, consider adding marula for an exotic twist. Cheers to the flavors of the African continent!

Chapter 3: Tamarind - The Origin and Distribution of Tamarind in Africa

Tamarind, scientifically known as Tamarindus indica, is a popular tropical fruit that has a wide range of culinary uses. Native to Africa, this delicious fruit is not only cherished for its unique tangy flavor but also holds significant cultural and historical importance in many African countries. In this chapter, we delve into the origin and distribution of tamarind in Africa, shedding light on its fascinating journey and the factors that have contributed to its wide presence across the continent.

The Origin of Tamarind in Africa:
The exact origin of tamarind in Africa remains a mystery, but it is widely believed to have originated in Sudan or tropical East Africa. Tamarind trees grow naturally in the savannas, from the northeast regions like Sudan, stretching through Ethiopia and down to southern Africa. With time, the seeds and knowledge of cultivating this versatile fruit spread throughout the continent.

Historical Significance:
Tamarind has a rich historical significance in many African cultures. It was highly valued for its medicinal properties, and ancient civilizations incorporated it into their traditional healing practices. Its high vitamin C content made it a sought-after remedy for ailments such as scurvy and coughs. Furthermore, tamarind was also revered for its ability to cool the body and reduce fever, especially during the hot African summers.

Distribution and Cultivation:
Over the centuries, tamarind cultivation spread across Africa due to various natural and human-driven factors. The fruit's ability to adapt to different climates, coupled with its nutritional benefits, made it popular among farmers and communities across the continent.

Today, tamarind trees can be found in numerous African countries, including Sudan, Ethiopia, Kenya, Uganda, Tanzania, Nigeria, Ghana, and Zimbabwe, among others. It thrives in regions with a tropical or arid climate, where it can withstand extreme heat and minimal rainfall. In addition to its growth in wild and natural conditions, tamarind is also cultivated in plantations, enriching the agricultural landscape of many African nations.

Culinary Delights and Traditional Uses:
Tamarind's unique flavor, with its distinctive sweet and sour taste, has made it a highly sought-after ingredient in African cuisine. From soups and stews to beverages and desserts, tamarind adds a delightful, tangy twist to many traditional dishes. In West Africa, for example, tamarind is a key ingredient in popular dishes such as "Shito," a spicy black sauce, and "Waakye," a local rice and bean dish.

Beyond gastronomy, tamarind has found its way into various cultural practices in Africa. In some communities, tamarind seeds are used as beads for jewelry, while the pulp can be fermented to produce alcoholic beverages. African folklore also associates tamarind with supernatural powers and fertility, making it an integral part of traditional rituals and ceremonies.

Tamarind's origin and distribution in Africa is a tale that intertwines history, culture, and agriculture. The fruit's versatility, delicious taste, and medicinal properties have made it an integral part of African societies for centuries. From its mysterious beginnings in the savannas of East Africa to its widespread cultivation across the continent, tamarind continues to captivate and enthrall both locals and visitors alike. Its journey represents the intricate tapestry of Africa's biodiversity, connecting diverse regions with a common love for this tangy treasure.

The uses and benefits of tamarind pulp and juice in Africa

Tamarind, a tropical fruit with a tangy taste, is widely known for its culinary uses in various cuisines across the world. In Africa, tamarind pulp and juice play a crucial role in enhancing the flavors of dishes and provide numerous health benefits. From culinary delights to traditional medicine, tamarind continues to be an integral part of African culture.

Tamarind, scientifically known as Tamarindus indica, is native to East Africa but has become naturalized in many parts of the continent. The fruit grows in abundance on trees and is harvested during the dry season. Its pulp is extracted from the long brown pods, which encase the fruit, and is packed with nutrients like vitamin C, B vitamins, potassium, magnesium, and antioxidants.

In African cuisine, tamarind pulp and juice are commonly used as natural souring agents, replaing vinegar or lemon juice. The tangy flavor of tamarind adds a unique taste to dishes, ranging from stews and sauces to marinades and chutneys. For instance, in West Africa, tamarind juice is a key ingredient in making the famous Senegalese dish "mafe"- a peanut sauce served over meat or vegetables. In East Africa, tamarind pulp is blended with spices to create a refreshing drink called "ukwaju."

Apart from its culinary uses, tamarind also offers several health benefits. It is a natural remedy for digestive issues due to its high fiber content and natural laxative properties. In many African households, tamarind is consumed to relieve constipation or used as a digestive aid. Tamarind also possesses anti-inflammatory properties that can help alleviate joint pain and reduce swelling caused by arthritis.

In traditional African medicine, tamarind is revered for its medicinal properties. Its bark, leaves, and roots are utilized to create herbal remedies for a variety of ailments. For instance, tamarind leaf juice is believed to have antibacterial properties and is used to treat wounds and prevent infections. In some parts of Africa, tamarind seeds powder is poulticed on the skin to treat boils and rashes.

Furthermore, tamarind pulp is often regarded as a remedy to combat fever. It is believed to reduce body temperature due to its cooling effect. The pulp is either consumed directly or used to make a refreshing drink to provide relief from the scorching heat during hot seasons.

In recent years, tamarind has gained attention for its potential in fighting malnutrition in Africa. Despite its tart taste, tamarind is an excellent source of essential nutrients and has been promoted as a nutritional supplement to curb vitamin deficiencies. It is especially rich in iron, making it a vital ingredient in combating anemia, a prevalent health issue on the continent.

Overall, the uses and benefits of tamarind pulp and juice in Africa are manifold. Whether it's enriching the flavors of regional cuisines, aiding digestion, serving as a traditional medicine, or fighting malnutrition, tamarind continues to play a significant role in African cultures and holds immense value in promoting both culinary delights and well-being on the continent.

- The examples and recipes of cocktails using tamarind in Africa

Africa is home to rich and diverse culinary traditions, with each region showcasing its own unique flavors and ingredients. One such ingredient, known for its tangy and sweet taste, is tamarind. Tamarind, with its roots in Africa, has been a staple ingredient in many dishes and beverages across the continent for centuries. Today, let's explore some of the refreshing cocktail recipes that incorporate this delightful ingredient.

1. Tamarind Mojito:

Ingredients:
- 2 tablespoons of fresh tamarind pulp
- 10 mint leaves
- Juice of 1 lime
- 2 teaspoons of sugar
- 2 ounces of white rum
- Soda Water

Instructions:
- In a glass, muddle the tamarind pulp, mint leaves, lime juice, and sugar until well combined.
- Add the rum and stir well.
- Fill the glass with ice and top it off with soda water.
- Garnish with a lime wedge and a sprig of mint. Enjoy!

2. Tamarind Margarita:
Ingredients:
- 2 ounces of silver tequila
- 1 tablespoon of tamarind concentrate
- Juice of 1 lime
- 1 ounce of triple sec
- Salt (for rimming the glass)
- Lime wedges (for garnish)

Instructions:
- Rim a glass with salt by running a lime slice around the edge and dipping it into salt.
- Fill the glass with ice cubes.
- In a shaker, combine tequila, tamarind concentrate, lime juice, and triple sec.
- Shake well and pour the mixture over ice.
- Garnish with a lime wedge and enjoy this tangy twist on a classic cocktail!

3. Tamarind Vodka Punch:
Ingredients:
- 1 cup of tamarind pulp
- 2 cups of water

- 1 cup of white sugar
- 1 cup of vodka
- Ice cubes
- Fresh mint leaves (for garnish)

Instructions:
- In a saucepan, combine tamarind pulp, water, and sugar. Bring the mixture to a boil, stirring occasionally until the sugar dissolves.
- Reduce the heat and let it simmer for 10-15 minutes, until the mixture thickens slightly.
- Remove from heat, strain the mixture to remove any remaining pulp, and let it cool completely.
- In a large pitcher, combine the tamarind mixture and vodka.
- Fill glasses with ice cubes and pour the tamarind vodka mixture over the ice.
- Garnish with a mint leaf and serve this refreshing punch at your gatherings.

These cocktail recipes beautifully showcase the versatility of tamarind, providing a balance of sweet and sour flavors that complement the African palate. Whether you want to cool down on a hot summer day or impress guests with unique flavors, these tamarind-based cocktails are sure to be a hit. So, gather your ingredients, mix up these delightful creations, and savor the taste of Africa with every sip!

Chapter 4: Hibiscus- The Origin and Distribution of Hibiscus in Africa

Hibiscus, often called the "queen of tropical flowers," is a vibrant and visually captivating plant species. Its extraordinary beauty and versatility have earned it a place in gardens, traditional medicine, and various cultural practices. In this chapter, we delve into the origin and distribution of hibiscus in Africa, unearthing captivating aspects of its history, cultural significance, and ecological adaptations across the continent.

1. Ancient African Origins:

The discovery of fossilized hibiscus pollen grains in sediment cores from the Sahara Desert provides evidence of hibiscus' antiquity in Africa. These pollen grains, dating back thousands of years, reveal the plant's existence in various regions across the continent during ancient times. It suggests that hibiscus has deep roots in Africa's natural ecosystem, stretching back to the prehistoric era.

2. Indigenous African Species:

Africa boasts an impressive diversity of indigenous hibiscus species, with many displaying unique characteristics and adaptations to their specific environments. For instance, the Hibiscus sabdariffa sub-species is endemic to West Africa, particularly Guinea, Cameroon, and Nigeria. It is best known for its distinct red calyx, which is commonly used to prepare a popular traditional beverage known as hibiscus tea or bissap.

South Africa is home to the Hibiscus Giganteus, a shrubby plant recognized for its sizeable single yellow flowers that bloom conspicuously throughout its flowering season. The Hibiscus rosa-sinensis, commonly known as the Chinese hibiscus, takes on various colors in its magnificent flowers, revealing the rich diversity present within Africa.

3. Cultural Significance:

Hibiscus holds significant cultural value in various African societies. Indigenous communities often embrace the plant in rituals, ceremonies, and traditional medicine. For instance, in ancient Egypt, hibiscus was symbolically linked to the fertility goddess, Hathor, and her sister, Nephthys. These goddesses were believed to provide blessings and protections, especially during childbirth and pregnancy.

In Nigeria, the hibiscus plant is an integral component of celebrations and festivals. Its vibrant petals are used to create exquisite floral decorations, symbolizing joy, beauty, and prosperity. Additionally, many traditional healers incorporate hibiscus in herbal remedies to address various ailments, showing the plant's significance in African traditional medicine.

4. Ecological Adaptations:

Hibiscus species across Africa have undergone unique adaptations to survive in diverse climatic conditions. Some sub-species, like the Hibiscus sabdariffa, have evolved mechanisms to endure the challenging drought conditions characteristic of many African regions. This adaptability has allowed hibiscus to thrive naturally, even in arid environments.

Furthermore, hibiscus plants in wetter tropical regions have evolved larger and more abundant leaves, enabling them to harness and utilize the abundant water resources more efficiently. Some species have even developed intricate root systems to withstand flooding during the rainy season, demonstrating their ability to adapt to dynamic environmental conditions.

The origin and distribution of hibiscus in Africa reveal its deep-rooted connections to the continent's past, its remarkable adaptability to varied ecological conditions, and its significant cultural significance. The captivating history, diverse species, and ecological adaptations of African hibiscus truly highlight the plant's unique place within the rich tapestry of the African continent.

- The uses and benefits of hibiscus flowers and tea in Africa

Hibiscus, known scientifically as Hibiscus sabdariffa, is a flowering plant native to Africa. The beautiful vibrant flowers of hibiscus are not only visually appealing but also offer numerous uses and benefits for the people of Africa. From making delicious herbal tea to providing essential health benefits, hibiscus flowers have become a significant part of African culture and livelihood.

One of the most popular uses of hibiscus flowers in Africa is to make hibiscus tea, also known as "sorrel" or "bissap" in different regions. The process involves steeping the dried hibiscus flowers in hot water, creating a refreshing, tart, ruby-red beverage. It is often served cold, sweetened with sugar or blended with other fruits for added flavor. Hibiscus tea has a tangy, cranberry-like taste, making it a favorite among many.

In traditional African folk medicine, hibiscus tea has long been used for its medicinal properties. The tea is rich in antioxidants such as polyphenols, flavonoids, and anthocyanins, which provide various health benefits. These antioxidants help protect the body against free radicals, lower inflammation, and support heart health. Hibiscus tea is also known for its potential to lower blood pressure and cholesterol levels, making it a natural remedy for hypertension and cardiovascular diseases, both of which are significant health issues in Africa.

Furthermore, hibiscus tea is considered a diuretic and has mild laxative properties, which can aid in digestion and alleviate constipation. It is often consumed after heavy meals to aid in digestion and promote overall gut health. In some African cultures, hibiscus tea is also believed to have aphrodisiac effects and is used as a natural remedy for various sexual ailments.

Aside from its health benefits, hibiscus flowers also have several other practical uses in African culture. The petals and calyx (the cup-like structure at the base of the flower) of hibiscus are used as dye sources, particularly in Sudanese, Nigerian, and Senegalese textiles. The vibrant red color obtained from hibiscus flowers is used for dyeing clothes, creating beautiful patterns that are characteristic of African fabric.

Moreover, hibiscus flowers are sometimes consumed as a food ingredient in Africa. The calyx is known for its tart flavor and is used in various traditional dishes such as jollof rice, soups, stews, and beverages. It imparts a tangy taste to the dishes and adds a visually pleasing element to the presentation.

The cultivation and use of hibiscus flowers in Africa also hold economic significance. It serves as a source of income for many farmers who grow hibiscus commercially and sell it to tea and dye manufacturers or exporters. The hibiscus industry provides employment opportunities and contributes to the economic growth of African countries.

In conclusion, hibiscus flowers and tea offer a multitude of uses and benefits in Africa. From brewing a refreshing beverage to promoting health and well-being, hibiscus has become an integral part of African culture and traditional medicine. Its versatile applications, such as dyeing textiles and adding flavor to food, contribute not only culturally but also economically to the growth of African nations.

- The examples and recipes of cocktails using hibiscus in Africa

Hibiscus is a vibrant and versatile flower that has long been a popular ingredient in cocktails across Africa. Known for its stunning crimson color, the hibiscus flower adds a unique and refreshing twist to traditional cocktail recipes. From the spicy flavors of North Africa to the fruity concoctions of the tropics, hibiscus cocktails are diverse and delicious. Here are a few examples and recipes of cocktails that incorporate hibiscus in African cuisine:

1. Bissap Cocktail (Senegal):
One of the most famous hibiscus cocktails in Africa is the Bissap cocktail, popular in Senegal. Bissap is derived from the name of the hibiscus flower, which is called "Roselle" in English. To make this cocktail, you will need:

- 2 cups of dried hibiscus petals
- 4 cups of water
- 1 cup of sugar
- Lime wedges for garnish
- Optional: rum, vodka, or gin (for alcoholic version)

Instructions:

1. Add the hibiscus petals and water to a large pot and bring it to a boil.
2. Let the mixture simmer for around 10 minutes, then remove it from heat and let it cool.
3. Once the mixture has cooled, strain out the hibiscus petals and discard them.
4. Add the sugar to the hibiscus liquid and stir until it dissolves.
5. Fill glasses with ice and pour the hibiscus liquid over the ice.
6. Squeeze a lime wedge into each glass for added citrus flavor.
7. Optional: Add a shot of rum, vodka, or gin to turn it into an alcoholic cocktail.
8. Stir well and garnish with additional lime wedges before serving.

2. Flamingo Fizz (Nigeria):
The Flamingo Fizz is a tropical hibiscus cocktail inspired by Nigerian flavors. It combines the tanginess of hibiscus with the sweetness of pineapple and the kick of ginger. To make this cocktail, you will need:

- 1 cup of hibiscus tea (brewed using dried hibiscus petals and water)

- 1 cup of pineapple juice
- 2 teaspoons of freshly grated ginger
- Juice of 1 lime
- Sparkling water
- Pineapple wedges and mint leaves for garnish

Instructions:

1. Brew a strong cup of hibiscus tea using dried hibiscus petals and water.
2. Let the tea cool down completely.
3. In a glass pitcher, combine the hibiscus tea, pineapple juice, grated ginger, and lime juice.
4. Stir well to combine all the flavors.
5. Fill glasses with ice and pour the mixture over the ice.
6. Top each glass with sparkling water to add fizz and excitement.
7. Garnish with pineapple wedges and mint leaves for a fresh and tropical touch.

3. Kilimanjaro Sunrise (Tanzania):
The Kilimanjaro Sunrise cocktail captures the vibrant and exotic flavors of Tanzania. This fruity and floral cocktail combines hibiscus tea with citrus and passion fruit. To make this cocktail, you will need:

- 1 cup of hibiscus tea (brewed using dried hibiscus petals and water)
- 1 cup of passion fruit juice
- Juice of 2 oranges
- 2 tablespoons of honey
- Ice cubes for serving
- Orange slices for garnish

Instructions:

1. Brew a cup of hibiscus tea using dried hibiscus petals and water.
2. Let the tea cool down.
3. In a shaker, combine the hibiscus tea, passion fruit juice, orange juice, and honey.
4. Shake well to mix all the ingredients.

5. Fill glasses with ice cubes and pour the cocktail over the ice.
6. Garnish each glass with an orange slice for a beautiful presentation.
7. Serve chilled and enjoy the flavor explosion in each sip.

These examples and recipes of hibiscus cocktails from Africa showcase the diverse range of flavors and creativity the continent has to offer. Whether you prefer a spicy and tangy Bissap cocktail or a fruity and exotic Kilimanjaro Sunrise, these recipes are sure to delight your taste buds and transport you to the vibrant cultures of Africa. So, raise a glass and toast to the bright and beautiful flavors of hibiscus in African cocktails!

Chapter 5: Ginger - The Origin and Distribution of Ginger in Africa

Ginger, scientifically known as Zingiber officinale, is a popular spice and herbal remedy with a long history of use in traditional medicine and culinary practices. In this chapter, we will explore the origin and distribution of ginger in Africa, shedding light on how this versatile plant found its way into the continent and has become an important part of its cultural and medicinal heritage.

1. Origins of Ginger:
Ginger is believed to have originated in Southeast Asia, specifically in the region between India and China. It was cultivated and traded extensively in ancient times, making its way through the Silk Road into different regions of the world. However, the precise route through which ginger reached Africa is still a subject of debate among botanists and historians.

2. Ancient Trade Routes:
Historical evidence suggests that Arabic traders, who were renowned for their maritime trading skills, played a crucial role in introducing ginger to Africa. From the series of ancient trade routes connecting the Arabian Peninsula to East Africa, ginger could have possibly been brought into the continent. Arab merchants would have transported ginger along with other valuable spices, herbs, and textiles during their journeys.

3. Medieval Spice Trade:
The medieval spice trade, with its epicenter in Egypt, also contributed to the distribution of ginger in Africa. Traders from Europe, Arab regions, and the Far East were involved in this large-scale commerce of spices, including ginger. As a result, ginger found its way into North Africa and gradually spread to the neighboring regions of the continent.

4. African Cultural Integration:

Once ginger arrived in Africa, it quickly gained popularity and became intertwined with local cultures and traditions. Ginger was not only appreciated as a flavoring agent in various dishes, but it also found its way into traditional medicine, where its medicinal properties were recognized and utilized by African traditional healers. Over time, ginger became deeply rooted in African society, its usage and cultivation evolving to match local customs.

5. Regional Distribution:
Ginger cultivation in Africa can be found across a wide range of climatic zones. In East Africa, countries like Tanzania, Kenya, and Uganda have suitable conditions for ginger farming, resulting in substantial production. West Africa, including Nigeria and Ghana, is another significant cultivating region. North African countries, such as Egypt and Morocco, have also embraced ginger cultivation, although in smaller quantities compared to their sub-Saharan counterparts. Overall, ginger has managed to spread and thrive in diverse African ecosystems.

6. Economic Significance:
The cultivation of ginger in Africa has both social and economic implications. Many African farmers rely on ginger farming as a source of income and livelihood. Additionally, the export of ginger has opened up avenues for economic growth and international trade. This lucrative export market has allowed African countries to establish themselves as major players in the global ginger trade.

7. Conservation Efforts and Challenges:
Despite the popularity of ginger in Africa, the conservation of this valuable spice plant is not without its challenges. Factors such as environmental degradation, pests, diseases, and global climate change pose threats to ginger cultivation in Africa. To tackle these challenges, efforts are being made to promote sustainable farming practices, develop disease-resistant varieties, and educate farmers about the importance of conservation.

The origin and distribution of ginger in Africa is an intriguing tale that highlights the continent's historical and cultural connections with the rest of the world. From its humble beginnings in Southeast Asia, ginger traveled through ancient trade routes, finding its way into Africa. Since then, it has become an intrinsic part of African cuisine and traditional medicine, contributing to the continent's cultural diversity. Its importance extends beyond culture, as ginger cultivation provides economic opportunities for African farmers and plays a vital role in the global spice trade. However, the challenges faced by ginger cultivation underscore the need for sustainable farming practices and conservation efforts to ensure its long-term viability in Africa.

- The uses and benefits of ginger root and beer in Africa

Ginger root and beer are two widely used and highly appreciated products in different regions of Africa. Both have been utilized for centuries due to their unique flavors and multitude of benefits. In this article, we will explore the many uses and benefits of ginger root and beer in Africa.

1. Ginger Root:
Ginger root, scientifically known as Zingiber officinale, is a perennial plant native to Southeast Asia. It holds immense cultural and medicinal value in Africa and is incorporated into various traditional remedies and cuisines. Here are some of the uses and benefits of ginger root in Africa:

Medical Uses:
- Anti-inflammatory properties: Ginger root has potent anti-inflammatory effects, which make it highly effective in treating joint pain and reducing inflammation in conditions such as arthritis. Many African traditional healers commonly use ginger root to alleviate pain.
- Digestive aid: Ginger root has long been used to alleviate gastrointestinal issues like nausea, bloating, and indigestion. It promotes the secretion of digestive enzymes, eases movement in the gastrointestinal tract, and relieves discomfort.

- Cold and flu remedy: Ginger root has natural anti-viral and immune-boosting properties. It is often used in traditional African medicine to treat ailments like colds, flu, and sore throat due to its ability to reduce inflammation and enhance immune response.

Culinary Uses:
- Flavor enhancer: Ginger root adds a distinctive spicy and refreshing flavor to African dishes and beverages. It is commonly included in soups, stews, curries, marinades, and teas, providing a unique taste that enhances the overall culinary experience.
- Food preservative: In some African cuisines, ginger root is incorporated into dishes as a natural preservative due to its antimicrobial properties, helping to inhibit the growth of bacteria and prolong food shelf life.
- Beverage ingredient: African cultures embrace ginger root in their traditional alcoholic and non-alcoholic beverages, ranging from ginger beer to ginger-infused teas. The use of ginger root enhances the flavor profiles, provides a natural carbonation effect, and contributes to the overall health benefits of the beverages.

2. Beer:
Beer holds a distinct place in African society and has been consumed for millennia. The traditional brewing methods and cultural significance vary across the continent, but the uses and benefits of beer in Africa remain consistent:

Cultural and Social Uses:
- Ceremonial celebrations: Beer plays a central role in many African traditional ceremonies, rituals, and social gatherings. It is often used to honor ancestral spirits, mark important events, and create a sense of community and togetherness among participants.
- Symbol of hospitality: Offering a glass of beer to guests is considered a token of hospitality and respect in various African cultures. Sharing beer is a way of building relationships and showing generosity.

Health and Nutritional Benefits:
- Nutrient-rich: Traditional African beer, such as sorghum beer or millet beer, is often brewed using cereals that provide important macronutrients

and micronutrients. These beers can serve as a dietary supplement, particularly in regions where malnutrition and micronutrient deficiencies are prevalent.
- Probiotic properties: Traditional African beer fermentation processes involve the use of various bacteria and yeasts, which contribute to natural probiotic qualities. Consuming probiotic-rich African beer can help maintain a healthy gut microbiome and improve digestion.

It is important to note that moderation is key when consuming both ginger root and beer, as excess intake can have adverse effects. Additionally, people with specific medical conditions or who are on certain medications should consult their healthcare providers before incorporating ginger root or beer into their diet.

In conclusion, the uses and benefits of ginger root and beer in Africa are extensive and deeply ingrained in the culture and traditions of the continent. Whether for its medicinal properties, culinary delights, or social significance, ginger root and beer continue to be valued and cherished by African communities.

- The examples and recipes of cocktails using ginger in Africa

Cocktails using ginger have become increasingly popular in Africa, and for good reason. This humble root brings a unique flavor and a myriad of health benefits to any drink it's added to. From refreshing ginger beers to creative ginger-infused spirits, the possibilities are endless. Let's explore some fantastic examples and recipes of cocktails using ginger in Africa.

1. Ginger Mojito:
Take a classic Mojito and give it a spicy twist with ginger. Start by muddling a few fresh mint leaves, a teaspoon of ginger syrup, and half a lime (juiced) in a glass. Add two ounces of white rum and fill the rest of the glass with ice.

Top it off with club soda and garnish with a sprig of mint and a lime wheel. This cocktail is perfect for those scorching summer afternoons.

2. Ginger Zinger:
This cocktail is for ginger aficionados who love a powerful kick. Begin by adding one ounce of ginger liqueur, half an ounce of ginger juice, and one and a half ounces of vodka into a shaker with ice. Shake vigorously and strain it into a chilled martini glass. Garnish it with a thin slice of ginger before serving.

3. African Ginger Presse:
This non-alcoholic cocktail is a delightful blend of ginger and fresh fruits. Begin by muddling a few raspberries, blueberries, and a slice of lemon in a glass. Add a tablespoon of ginger syrup, fill the glass with ice, and top it off with ginger beer. Stir gently and garnish with a lemon twist for a vibrant, refreshing drink.

4. Ginger Margarita:
Give the classic Margarita a spicy African twist by adding ginger syrup and chili powder. Start by rimming a glass with the chili powder and filling it with ice. In a shaker, combine two ounces of tequila, one ounce of lime juice, and half an ounce of ginger syrup. Shake vigorously and strain it into the prepared glass. Garnish with a lime wedge and fresh ginger slice.

5. Spicy Ginger Sangria:
Impress your guests with an African-inspired ginger sangria. Begin by muddling a few slices of granny smith apples, oranges, and cinnamon sticks in a large pitcher. Add one cup of pineapple juice, half a cup of ginger liqueur, and half a cup of orange liqueur. Mix well and refrigerate for at least two hours. Just before serving, add a bottle of red wine and ginger ale. Pour it into individual glasses filled with ice and garnish with a sprig of fresh mint.

Remember to adjust the amount of ginger to suit your taste preferences. These cocktail recipes are merely starting points to inspire your own creativity. Bring the warmth and freshness of ginger to your African-inspired drinks and savor the lively flavors they offer. Cheers to the power of ginger and its ability to transform a cocktail into a truly memorable experience.

Chapter 6: Rooibos - The Origin and Distribution of Rooibos in South Africa

6.1 Introduction

In this chapter, we delve into the captivating story of rooibos, a unique indigenous South African herbal tea. We explore its origins and the history of its distribution within the country. Rooibos, also known as Red Bush tea, has gained global popularity in recent years due to its remarkable health benefits and delicious taste. However, to truly appreciate rooibos, it is essential to understand its humble beginnings and the defining characteristics that make it one of the most treasured teas worldwide.

6.2 The Origins of Rooibos

Rooibos is derived from the Aspalathus linearis plant, which is native to the rugged Cederberg region of the Western Cape province in South Africa. The plant has thrived for centuries in this specific geographical area due to its unique climatic conditions. The Cederberg region experiences mild winters and hot, dry summers, creating the perfect environment for rooibos to grow and flourish.

Indigenous Khoi and San tribes, who inhabited the Cederberg region long before European explorers arrived, were the first to discover the remarkable characteristics of rooibos. They would collect the leaves, stems, and flowers of the plant, lightly bruise them, and then allow them to ferment in the sun. This fermentation process catalyzed a crucial chemical change within the leaves, imparting the distinct red color and enhancing the flavor profile of the tea.

6.3 The Spread of Rooibos in South Africa

While rooibos primarily thrived in the Cederberg region, it eventually captured the attention of neighboring communities. Word of its unique taste and health benefits spread rapidly, leading to increased demand for the tea. As a result, rooibos cultivation gradually spread further afield and became an important agricultural activity in the surrounding areas.

The establishment of Nieuwoudtville, in the Bokkeveld region, marked an important milestone in the expansion of rooibos cultivation. Here, farmers seized the opportunity to grow rooibos on a larger scale and developed innovative methods to improve cultivation techniques. They experimented with various rooibos hybrids, aiming to enhance the quality and production yield of the tea. This marked the beginning of consistent and significant development in rooibos cultivation.

6.4 Commercialization and Global Reach

It was not until the late 19th century that rooibos faced its most significant transformative moment. Two enterprising German settlers, Benjamin Ginsberg and Carl Humberg, recognized the potential of rooibos as a commercially viable product. They started cultivating rooibos on a large scale and marketed it as a herbal tea to both local and international consumers.

The journey to global recognition emerged during the early 20th century, with European consumers developing a fondness for this strikingly red and aromatic tea. Rooibos transcended its traditional uses and soon became a staple in many countries across Europe. South Africa's export industry benefited from this surge in demand, with rooibos cultivation expanding rapidly to meet international orders.

6.5 Regulation and Protection

Recognizing the significance of rooibos to South African culture, the country's government took proactive steps to protect and regulate the production of this South African gem. In 1998, the South African Rooibos Council was established to guide and oversee the industry, ensuring sustainability while maintaining the authenticity of South African rooibos.

As rooibos continues to stake its claim on the global tisane market, it remains deeply linked to its roots in South African culture and indigenous history. The Cederberg region still stands as the heartland of rooibos cultivation, where generations of farmers utilize careful harvesting and fermentation techniques, passed down through the ages, to maintain the tea's invaluable characteristics.

6.6 Future Possibilities

The future of rooibos's evolution remains promising, with ongoing research into its valuable health properties and potential applications in beauty and skincare products. As consumer interest in natural and sustainable lifestyle choices continues to grow, rooibos finds itself poised for even greater recognition on the global stage.

In the next chapter, we dive deeper into the remarkable health benefits that have propelled rooibos to international fame. From its abundance of antioxidants to its potential in combating various ailments, rooibos proves to be both tasty and exceptionally good for you.

- The uses and benefits of rooibos leaves and tea in South Africa

Rooibos, also known as "redbush" tea, is a herbal beverage that originates from the Western Cape region of South Africa. It is made from the leaves of the plant Aspalathus linearis and has gained popularity not just in South Africa but around the world due to its unique flavor, numerous health benefits, and versatility in culinary uses.

One of the most significant benefits of rooibos lies in its high antioxidant content. Antioxidants are compounds that protect the body against free radicals, which can cause oxidative stress and contribute to various chronic diseases. Rooibos contains a range of antioxidants, including aspalathin and nothofagin, which have been linked to reduced inflammation and improved heart health.

Consuming rooibos tea has also been associated with improved digestion. It contains several compounds that can help reduce stomach ailments such as indigestion, nausea, and diarrhea. In particular, rooibos has been found to contain antispasmodic agents that relax the digestive muscles, alleviating discomfort.

Furthermore, rooibos has beneficial effects on the skin. It is rich in alpha hydroxy acid and zinc, which promote a healthy complexion by reducing signs of aging, soothing acne-prone skin, and aiding in the healing of scars and blemishes. Many South African skincare products incorporate rooibos extracts for their natural skincare properties.

In addition to its health benefits, rooibos tea is enjoyed for its delicious taste. It is naturally sweet, with earthy and slightly nutty undertones, making it a pleasant drink on its own or blended with other flavors. It can be served hot or cold and is a popular choice as a caffeine-free alternative to black or green tea. Rooibos blends well with various ingredients such as fruits, herbs, and spices, further adding to its versatility.

Moreover, the cultivation and processing of rooibos have important socioeconomic benefits in South Africa. Rooibos farming creates employment opportunities for many local communities, particularly in the Cederberg region where the plant thrives. The industry supports thousands of small-scale farmers who sustainably cultivate and harvest the leaves, preserving the local ecosystem and biodiversity.

Rooibos has also provided economic empowerment for the indigenous Khoisan people, who have been harvesting and using the leaves for centuries. The South African government recognizes rooibos as a traditional product and has granted Protected Geographic Indicator (PGI) status to guarantee its origin and quality. This protects the local farmers and ensures that the benefits from the tea's popularity reach those who have been involved in its production for generations.

Overall, the uses and benefits of rooibos leaves and tea are extensive. From its potent antioxidants and digestive properties to its positive impact on the skin, rooibos offers both a flavorful and healthy choice for tea enthusiasts. The sustainable cultivation of rooibos not only supports local communities and preserves the environment but also celebrates centuries of indigenous knowledge and cultural heritage in South Africa.

- The examples and recipes of cocktails using rooibos in South Africa

In recent years, the popularity of rooibos has skyrocketed as more people become aware of its health benefits and unique flavor profile. Originating from the Western Cape province of South Africa, rooibos (also known as red bush tea) is a herbal infusion made from the leaves of the Aspalathus linearis plant. Besides being enjoyed as a soothing beverage, rooibos has found a place behind the bar as mixologists experiment with its distinct taste in a variety of cocktails. In this article, we will delve into some of the examples and recipes of cocktails using rooibos in South Africa, offering a tantalizing fusion of traditional and contemporary concoctions.

One of the most iconic cocktails to feature rooibos is the "African Sunrise." This vibrant and refreshing drink perfectly captures the vibrant colors of a sunset in the African savannah. To create this cocktail, combine freshly brewed rooibos tea (cooled) with vodka, cranberry juice, and a splash of sparkling water. Garnish with a slice of orange or a sprig of mint for added visual appeal. The African Sunrise is a crowd-pleasing option, highlighting the rich flavor and earthy undertones of rooibos.

For those looking for a more decadent experience, the "Spiced Rooibos Martini" is a must-try. Infused with warm, aromatic spices, this cocktail takes the unique flavors of rooibos to new heights. To make this indulgent martini, start by steeping rooibos tea with a cinnamon stick, cloves, and a touch of vanilla. Allow the tea to cool before mixing it with vodka, a dash of honey or maple syrup, and a squeeze of lemon juice. Serve in a chilled martini glass and garnish with a sprinkle of ground cinnamon or a cinnamon stick for an added touch of elegance.

For those who prefer a sweeter profile, the "Rooibos Mojito" offers a delightful twist on the classic Cuban cocktail. Begin by muddling fresh mint leaves, lime wedges, and a teaspoon of sugar in a glass. Prepare a strong rooibos tea and allow it to cool before pouring it into the glass. Add a generous splash of rum and crushed ice, then stir gently to combine all the flavors. Top it off with a splash of soda water and garnish with a mint sprig and a lime wheel, presenting a visually appealing and refreshing cocktail.

When exploring rooibos cocktails, it's important to keep in mind that this unique ingredient can be incorporated into various other mixed drinks, including those typically not associated with tea. For instance, rooibos pairs exceptionally well with gin, creating a fragrant and complex base for cocktails such as a rooibos-infused Negroni or a rooibos and elderflower gin fizz. These cocktails not only showcase the versatility of rooibos but also unleash a whole new world of flavors and textures.

As you dive into the world of cocktails using rooibos in South Africa, don't be afraid to experiment with your own flavor combinations. Whether you're a skilled mixologist or a beginner enthusiast, rooibos offers endless possibilities for unique and exciting cocktails that celebrate the rich cultural heritage of South Africa while exploring new frontiers in mixology. So raise your glass and toast to the taste of rooibos, a versatile and enticing ingredient that continues to captivate people all around the globe.

Chapter 7: Coffee - The Origin and Distribution of Coffee in Africa

In this chapter, we will delve into the fascinating history of coffee, exploring its origins and distribution in the vast continent of Africa. Coffee, a beverage enjoyed by millions of people globally, has a rich history that intertwines with the culture, economies, and societies of various African nations. It is essential to know the journey coffee took to reach its current status, as it provides valuable insights into Africa's agricultural and trade systems.

Origins of Coffee in Africa:
The story of coffee begins in Ethiopia, specifically in the region known as Kaffa, which is believed to be the birthplace of coffee. According to legend, a goat herder named Kaldi noticed his goats becoming lively and energetic after consuming berries from a particular tree. Curiosity piqued, Kaldi tried the berries himself and experienced their invigorating effects. Word of this discovery soon spread, leading to the cultivation and propagation of coffee.

Cultivation and Various Species:
As coffee gained popularity in Ethiopia, its cultivation techniques developed, leading to the establishment of coffee plantations throughout the country. Ethiopia boasts an array of unique coffee species, each with distinct flavors and characteristics. These species include Arabica, the most prevalent and highly sought-after globally, as well as varieties like Kaffa, Harar, Sidamo, and Yirgacheffe. The diverse coffee species found in Ethiopia capture the essence of Africa's coffee legacy.

Spreading Through the Continent:
Coffee made its way from Ethiopia into neighboring countries through various means, such as explorations, trade routes, and colonization. The Arab merchants, known for their influential trading networks, played a significant role in spreading coffee across the continent. The coffee trees thrived in the conducive climates and soil conditions found throughout

Africa, making it favorable for coffee plantations to expand.

Notable Coffee-Producing Countries in Africa:
Today, several African countries have established themselves as major contributors to the global coffee market. Ethiopia, the birthplace of coffee, continues to be among the leading African coffee producers. Its unique blend of coffee resources, such as the elevation, climate, soil, and distinct varieties, keep Ethiopian coffee highly sought-after and esteemed.

Other notable coffee-producing countries in Africa include Uganda, where coffee farming has played a key role in its economy, as well as Kenya, which has gained a reputation for its meticulously cultivated and processed coffee beans. Other countries such as Tanzania, Rwanda, Burundi, and the Democratic Republic of Congo are also emerging as notable coffee producers, capturing attention with their distinct flavors and high-quality beans.

Impacts on Economies and Communities:
The coffee industry has had profound economic and social impacts on African countries. For many coffee-producing nations, coffee exports contribute significantly to their economies, providing income, employment, and foreign exchange. Coffee farming has become a vital source of livelihood for numerous communities, helping to alleviate poverty and improve living conditions.

Moreover, regional coffee cooperatives and organizations have emerged, empowering farmers, promoting sustainable practices, and fostering fair trade. By supporting ethical and environmentally friendly production, African coffee produces a positive ripple effect throughout society.

The origins and distribution of coffee in Africa exhibit the continent's timeless connection with this beloved beverage. From its humble beginnings in Ethiopia to its cultivation and diverse varieties found throughout various nations, Africa has shaped the global coffee industry. Understanding the rich history of coffee in Africa not only allows us to appreciate this extraordinary drink but also sheds light on important social, economic, and environmental narratives embedded within its cultivation.

- The uses and benefits of coffee beans and brew in Africa

The Uses and Benefits of Coffee Beans and Brew in Africa

Coffee constitutes a significant part of daily life, celebrated for its rich aroma, intense flavor, and stimulating effects. Africa, often referred to as the birthplace of coffee, has a long-standing tradition of cultivating coffee beans and cherishing its brew. This article aims to delve into the uses and benefits of coffee beans and the brewing culture in various African regions.

1. Historical Significance and Regional Varieties:
Coffee cultivation has a deep-rooted history in Africa, where it was discovered centuries ago. Ethiopia, specifically the Kaffa region, is believed to be the homeland of coffee. African coffee is renowned for its high quality and diverse flavors, showcasing distinct regional characteristics. Prominent African coffee varieties include Ethiopian Harrar, Kenyan AA, Tanzanian Peaberry, Rwandan Bourbon, and more.

2. Economic Importance:
Coffee plays a vital role in the African economy, providing a significant source of income for many communities. In countries such as Ethiopia, Uganda, and Kenya, coffee farming supports thousands of small-scale farmers and their families, enabling economic growth and poverty reduction. This crop contributes to foreign exchange earnings and offers opportunities for trade and investment in the global market.

3. Health Benefits:
Aside from being a popular beverage, coffee offers several health benefits

when consumed in moderation. African studies have highlighted its potential advantages, including improved cognitive function, reduced risk of liver disease, and increased antioxidant intake. Additionally, coffee consumption has been associated with a lower risk of depression, Parkinson's disease, type 2 diabetes, and some types of cancer.

4. Cultural Significance:
Coffee holds great cultural significance in various parts of Africa, often being an integral part of social gatherings and ceremonies. In Ethiopia, coffee ceremonies are widely practiced, symbolizing a gesture of friendship, hospitality, and cultural identity. This ritual involves roasting, grinding, brewing, and serving coffee in traditional clay jugs, representing community and connection.

5. Culinary Uses:
Coffee possesses diverse culinary applications across Africa. It is commonly used as an ingredient in traditional recipes, lending a distinct flavor to savory dishes like stews, marinades, and spice rubs. In Ethiopia, coffee-infused butter is a popular addition to various pastry and bread preparations, elevating the taste profile and invoking nostalgia.

6. Beverage Industry and Specialty Coffee:
Africa is instrumental in supplying a substantial percentage of the world's coffee, and its contribution extends beyond exportation. Many African countries are witnessing a boom in the specialty coffee industry, focusing on high-quality, traceable, and sustainable production. This niche market highlights the unique characteristics of African coffee, fostering economic growth and promoting direct relationships between farmers, exporters, and roasters worldwide.

The uses and benefits of coffee beans and brew in Africa go beyond the realms of a daily beverage. Rooted in the continent's history, geography, and cultural traditions, coffee offers economic opportunities, health benefits, and culinary enhancements. As the love for African specialty coffee continues to grow, it elevates the global appreciation of African coffee farmers' dedication and craftsmanship, ensuring a sustainable future for this beloved caffeinated treasure.

- The examples and recipes of cocktails using coffee in Africa

When it comes to delicious and flavorful cocktails, coffee is often overlooked as a key ingredient. However, in Africa, where coffee bean production is thriving, this rich and aromatic beverage is finding its way into unique and delectable cocktails that are sure to satisfy even the most discerning palate. From classic coffee-based cocktails to creative combinations involving indigenous ingredients, African mixologists are pushing boundaries and showcasing the versatility of coffee in cocktail culture. Here, we will explore some examples and recipes of cocktails using coffee in Africa, leaving your taste buds yearning for more.

1. Ethiopian Espresso Martini:
As the birthplace of coffee, Ethiopia offers a feast of coffee-inspired beverages. This exotic twist on the classic espresso martini infuses the robust flavor of Ethiopian coffee into the mix. To create this delightful concoction, combine a shot of Ethiopian espresso, one ounce of vodka, half an ounce of coffee liqueur, and a splash of simple syrup. Shake vigorously over ice and strain into a martini glass. Don't forget to garnish with coffee beans for that extra touch of elegance.

2. Moroccan Spiced Coffee Cocktail:
To add a touch of North African flair to your cocktail repertoire, try this Moroccan-inspired coffee blend. Begin by brewing a strong pot of Moroccan-style spiced coffee featuring elements like cardamom, cloves, cinnamon, and ginger. Allow the coffee to cool, then mix it with an equal amount of vanilla vodka and a dash of chocolate liqueur for richness. Shake the mixture with ice and strain it into a coffee-rimmed cocktail glass for a visually captivating treat.

3. Tanzanian Coffee Margarita:
Take a tropical getaway with this Tanzanian twist on a classic margarita. In a shaker, combine two ounces of tequila, one ounce of freshly brewed Tanzanian coffee, one ounce of lime juice, half an ounce of agave syrup, and a handful of ice. Shake vigorously and strain the mixture into a salt-rimmed glass filled with fresh ice. For that final touch of Caribbean island vibes, garnish your creation with a lime wheel and a sprig of mint.

4. South African Africanized Espresso Martini:
Embrace the diverse flavors of South Africa by incorporating their beloved "Rooibos" tea into an espresso martini. Start by brewing a mixture of strong espresso and Rooibos tea (1:1 ratio) and letting it cool. Blend an ounce of the coffee-tea concoction with two ounces of vodka, half an ounce of coffee liqueur, and a sprinkle of cinnamon. Shake well in a cocktail shaker filled with ice, and strain it into a chilled martini glass. The result is a harmonious marriage of coffee, tea, and spicy sweetness.

5. Kenyan Coffee Dawa:
In Swahili, Dawa means "medicine," and this Kenyan cocktail is rumored to cure anything from a hangover to a broken heart. Begin by muddling lime wedges and a teaspoon of brown sugar in a glass. Add a shot of Kenyan coffee, a splash of vodka, and fill the glass with crushed ice. Stir well, ensuring the sugar dissolves, and garnish with fresh mint and a sprinkle of ground coffee beans. Sip slowly, savoring the unique blend of citrus, sweetness, and coffee.

These examples of coffee-infused cocktails from various African regions highlight the extraordinary versatility of coffee as a mixer. Whether you appreciate the bold flavors of Ethiopian espresso or the earthy richness of Tanzanian coffee, incorporating coffee into cocktails adds depth and character to familiar recipes. So step into the realm of African coffee cocktails and be prepared to embark on a flavor-filled journey through the continent's diverse coffee culture.

Chapter 8: Cocoa - The Origin and Distribution of Cocoa in Africa

Cocoa, scientifically known as Theobroma cacao, is a tropical tree native to the rainforests of Central and South America. However, its cultivation and production have extended beyond its original habitat and now Africa is known to be the largest cocoa-producing region in the world. This chapter explores the fascinating history and distribution of cocoa in Africa, shedding light on how this beloved crop became an integral part of the continent's agricultural landscape.

The Arrival of Cocoa in Africa:

Cocoa was introduced to Africa by the European colonizers during the 18th Century. It is believed that the first cocoa trees were planted in the island of Sao Tomé off the West African coast, which served as a major colonial trading post. The Portuguese, who were particularly active in the region, were responsible for bringing cocoa seeds and establishing plantations in their colonies.

From Sao Tomé, cocoa cultivation quickly spread to neighboring regions such as Ghana, Nigeria, and Cameroon. The favorable climate, fertile soils, and an abundance of rainforest areas in these regions proved ideal for cocoa production. Thus, cocoa plantations thrived and provided a lucrative income for both colonial powers and local farmers.

Cocoa Market Expansion:

By the late 19th century, the demand for cocoa skyrocketed, primarily fueled by European chocolate manufacturers. As a result, African countries witnessed explosive growth in their cocoa production. Ghana became the leading cocoa producer globally, earning it the title "Gold Coast," reflecting the immense wealth generated from this crop.

The distribution of cocoa plantations in Africa expanded further during the 20th century. Ivory Coast emerged as Ghana's main competitor, controlling a significant share of the cocoa market. Other West African countries, including Nigeria, Cameroon, Sierra Leone, and Liberia, also established themselves as key cocoa-producing nations.

Effects on Local Economies and Societies:

The establishment of cocoa plantations in Africa not only transformed economic landscapes but also had extensive social implications. As cocoa farming attracted a large number of rural farmers, the industry played a crucial role in providing job opportunities and income for rural communities. Consequently, migration from rural to cocoa-growing areas increased, leading to the formation of new settlements and villages.

Furthermore, cocoa production often involved complex webs of trade, involving cooperatives, intermediaries, and processing industries. This interconnectivity created a dynamic market, boosting local economies and fostering cross-border trade between cocoa-producing countries.

Challenges and Sustainability in Cocoa Distribution:

Despite being the world's largest cocoa producer, African countries face numerous challenges in the distribution of cocoa. One of the main issues is maintaining quality and reducing post-harvest losses. Infrastructure limitations, such as poor storage facilities, lack of efficient transportation networks, and improper handling techniques, lead to significant losses and affect the overall quality of cocoa beans.

Additionally, environmental concerns such as climate change, deforestation, and limited access to resources like water and fertilizers pose further threats to cocoa sustainability in Africa. However, several initiatives by international organizations, governments, and the cocoa industry itself aim to address these challenges and promote sustainable cocoa production in the region.

The story of cocoa in Africa is a testament to the resilience and adaptability of this crop. From its humble beginnings on the shores of Sao Tomé to becoming the backbone of West Africa's agriculture, cocoa has embedded itself deeply in the economies and societies of African nations. With ongoing efforts towards sustainability and quality improvement, the future of cocoa in Africa looks promising, ensuring that this extraordinary crop continues to shape the region's history and contribute to the joy and delight of chocolate lovers worldwide.

- The uses and benefits of cocoa beans and chocolate in Africa

The Uses and Benefits of Cocoa Beans and Chocolate in Africa

Cocoa beans and chocolate are widely celebrated for their delectable taste and luxurious qualities. However, their importance extends far beyond people's indulgence in sweets. In Africa, cocoa beans play a fundamental role in the economy, culture, and wellbeing of countless communities. This article explores the fascinating and diverse uses as well as the impactful benefits of cocoa beans and chocolate in Africa.

1. Economic Growth:
Cocoa production is a major source of income for numerous African countries, contributing significantly to their economic growth and development. As one of Africa's primary export commodities, cocoa has consistently generated revenue for communities, created employment opportunities, and facilitated foreign exchange earnings.

2. Small-scale Farming:
Cocoa cultivation in Africa predominantly relies on small-scale farming, with millions of farmers involved in its production. This empowers local

communities by providing income-generating activities and promoting sustainable agricultural practices.

3. Nutritional Value:
Cocoa beans, in their raw form, are highly nutritious. Packed with polyphenols, flavonoids, minerals, and vitamins, cocoa beans contribute to a balanced diet. Rich in antioxidants, cocoa offers various health benefits, including improved cardiovascular function and reduced risk of certain diseases.

4. Cottage Industries:
The processing of cocoa beans into chocolate has given rise to cottage industries across Africa. From local chocolate makers to craft chocolatiers, these businesses create value-added products, shining a spotlight on African gastronomy and increasing tourism opportunities.

5. Employment Generation:
The expansion of the cocoa industry in Africa has created numerous employment opportunities, primarily in rural areas where job opportunities may be limited. This ensures that people within cocoa-producing regions have sustainable means of income, thus reducing poverty and improving livelihoods.

6. Infrastructure Development:
Cocoa cultivation often requires significant investments in infrastructure, including transportation, storage facilities, and processing plants. This development translates into improved infrastructure not only for the cocoa sector but also for the overall well-being of communities, enabling easier access to education, healthcare, and marketplaces.

7. Cultural Significance:
Cocoa beans have a rich cultural significance in Africa. For centuries, they have been used in various rituals, celebrations, and medicinal remedies. The beans hold a special place in African heritage, reflecting the cultural diversity and traditions of different communities.

8. Value Chain Development:

Cocoa production in Africa spans the entire value chain, from farming to processing, manufacturing, and marketing. By investing in this value chain, African countries can move away from exporting solely raw beans, unlocking opportunities for higher returns through value addition and capturing a larger share of the global market.

9. Foreign Exchange Earnings:
Due to its high market demand, cocoa and chocolate provide African countries with substantial foreign exchange earnings. This revenue enables governments to invest in infrastructure, education, healthcare, and other socio-economic sectors crucial for human development.

It is evident that cocoa beans and chocolate have become integral to the fabric of African societies, providing economic opportunities, health benefits, and preserving unique cultural traditions. By recognizing and tapping into their potential, Africa can continue to harness the power of cocoa to drive sustainable development, adding sweetness to both palates and lives across the continent.

- The examples and recipes of cocktails using cocoa in Africa

Exquisite Cocoa-Inspired African Cocktails- Recipes and Examples

Africa is not only known for its breathtaking landscapes and vibrant cultures but also for its unique and diverse culinary traditions. A lesser-known aspect of African gastronomy is the inclusion of cocoa, a versatile and rich ingredient that adds a delightful twist to cocktail recipes. In this article, we will explore a range of examples and recipes showcasing the fascinating use of cocoa in African cocktails.

1. Chocolate Martini:
Ingredients:
- 2 oz vodka
- 1 oz chocolate liqueur
- 1 oz cream liqueur
- 1 tbsp cocoa powder
- Chocolate shavings (for garnish)

Instructions:
- Rim a chilled cocktail glass with cocoa powder.
- In a shaker, combine the vodka, chocolate liqueur, cream liqueur, and cocoa powder.
- Shake vigorously and strain the mixture into the prepared glass.
- Garnish with chocolate shavings, and serve chilled.

2. Moroccan Spiced Cocoa Cocktail:
Ingredients:
- 1½ oz cocoa-infused rum
- 1 oz spiced simple syrup
- 1 tbsp fresh lemon juice
- ½ cup milk
- Star anise (for garnish)

Instructions:
- In a shaker, combine the cocoa-infused rum, spiced simple syrup, lemon juice, and milk.
- Shake well with ice until frothy.
- Strain into a rocks glass filled with ice.
- Garnish with a star anise, and enjoy.

3. African Mocha Martini:
Ingredients:
- 2 oz coffee liqueur
- 1½ oz vodka
- 2 tsp cocoa powder
- 2 oz strong brewed African coffee
- Chocolate-covered espresso beans (for garnish)

Instructions:
- Prepare two espresso shots using the African coffee and let them cool.

- In a shaker, combine the coffee liqueur, vodka, cocoa powder, and cooled espresso shots.
- Shake vigorously and strain the mixture into a chilled martini glass.
- Garnish with chocolate-covered espresso beans.

4. Ghanaian Hot Chocolate Cocktail:
Ingredients:
- 1½ oz bourbon
- 1½ oz milk chocolate liqueur
- 1 cup hot chocolate
- Whipped cream
- Shaved dark chocolate (for garnish)

Instructions:
- In a heatproof glass, combine the bourbon, milk chocolate liqueur, and hot chocolate.
- Stir well until combined.
- Top with whipped cream and garnish with shaved dark chocolate.
- Serve immediately while still hot.

Africa boasts countless flavors and ingredients cherished worldwide, and cocoa is undoubtedly one of them. By incorporating cocoa into cocktail recipes, the continent offers a unique twist to the world of mixology. The provided examples and recipes inspire creativity in utilizing cocoa's rich and aromatic profile, adding a delightful touch to African-themed gatherings or cozy nights spent indulging in these delectable cocoa-infused beverages. Cheers to enjoying the enchanting fusion of Africa's cocoa and mixology!

Chapter 9: Mint - The Origin and Distribution of Mint in Africa

Mint, a highly aromatic perennial herb, holds a special place in the hearts and homes of people around the world. Used in various culinary and medicinal applications, mint is popular for its refreshing flavor and numerous health benefits. In this chapter, we delve into the origin and distribution of mint in Africa, exploring its rich history, cultural significance, and geographic patterns of growth.

1. Historical Significance:

Mint's historical roots run deep in Africa, with evidence of its presence dating back thousands of years. Ancient Egyptians considered mint sacred and valued it for its versatile uses. The Egyptians utilized mint as a healing herb, refreshing ingredient in cosmetics, and symbols of hospitality for their honored guests.

2. Geographic Distribution:

Africa boasts a diverse range of climates, landscapes, and ecosystems, contributing to the varied distribution of mint species across the continent. Mint, as a herb, prefers well-drained soils and thrives in warm environments with ample sunlight.

In the northern parts of Africa, various species of mint, such as Mentha aquatica and Mentha spicata, can be found growing in regions with a Mediterranean climate. These areas, including Morocco, Tunisia, and Egypt, provide ideal conditions for mint growth, with mild winters, moderate rainfall, and warm summers.

Moving towards the eastern part of the continent, in countries like Ethiopia and Kenya, mint is grown predominantly in the highlands where cool temperatures and ample water supply create favorable conditions for its cultivation.

As we shift to equatorial regions, such as Uganda, Tanzania, and the Democratic Republic of Congo, one can find different types of mint cultivated in cooler mountainous regions, receiving abundant rainfall throughout the year.

3. Traditional Uses:

Mint holds great cultural significance across Africa, being integrated into local cuisines, traditional medicines, and spiritual rituals. Due to its cooling nature, mint-infused drinks are popular for providing respite from the hot African climate. In countries like Egypt and Morocco, mint tea, often sweetened with sugar or honey, is an integral part of the social fabric and is generously served to guests as a symbol of hospitality.

Across the continent, mint's medicinal properties are widely recognized. Mint leaves can be chewed to alleviate headaches, stomach ailments, and respiratory problems. Traditional healers in various African communities consider mint as a potent remedy for digestive disorders, nausea, and heartburn.

4. Commercial Cultivation:

In recent years, the commercial cultivation and global trade of mint from Africa have gained significant momentum. The abundant availability of raw materials, combined with favorable climatic conditions, has attracted attention from the international market.

Egypt remains one of the largest producers and exporters of mint-derived products, including mint oils, dried mint leaves, and mint essence. The country possesses not only favorable growing conditions but also well-established infrastructure for mint harvesting, processing, and refinement.

In countries like Morocco and Tunisia, specialized farming practices and traditional knowledge have propelled the production of high-quality organic mint products, catering to the rising demand for natural and sustainable alternatives in global markets.

The origin and distribution of mint in Africa reveal a fascinating interplay between geography, culture, and historical significance. From ancient Egypt's reverence for the herb to present-day commercial cultivation, mint continues to flourish in the diverse regions of Africa.

The enchanting aroma of mint wafts through the continent's landscapes, enriching cuisines, promoting health benefits, and connecting individuals through the shared love for this versatile herb. As Africa's influence in the global market expands, so too will its contribution to the global mint industry, making it a vital player in providing the world with this aromatic treasure.

- The uses and benefits of mint leaves and oil in Africa

Mint leaves and oil have been widely used in various cultures around the world for centuries. In Africa, they have also found extensive applications due to their numerous uses and benefits. This article will delve into the uses and benefits of mint leaves and oil in Africa, shedding light on their traditional and medicinal practices.

Firstly, mint leaves are commonly used in African cuisine. They add a distinct flavor and aroma to dishes, making them a popular herb in culinary preparations. Mint leaves are a key ingredient in traditional dishes such as Moroccan tea, Egyptian karkade, and Nigerian peppermint tea. The refreshing taste of mint complements the savory, sweet, and tangy flavors of African cuisine, enhancing the gastronomic experience.

Moreover, mint leaves are known for their diverse medicinal properties. In Africa, they have been utilized for their therapeutic benefits for centuries. One of the primary uses of mint leaves is to alleviate digestive issues. Mint leaves possess natural antispasmodic properties, which helps in relieving cramps, flatulence, and bloating. Infusions made from mint leaves are often consumed to soothe gastrointestinal discomfort and promote healthy digestion.

Furthermore, mint leaves are commonly used to treat respiratory ailments and promote respiratory health. The menthol component present in mint leaves acts as a decongestant, relieving respiratory congestion and promoting clearer breathing. In many African cultures, mint leaves are brewed as teas or inhaled as vapors to alleviate symptoms of cough, cold, and sinusitis.

In addition to mint leaves, mint oil is also a widely used and highly valued product in Africa. One of its major applications is in the field of aromatherapy. Mint oil is known for its invigorating and refreshing scent, which has a rejuvenating effect on the mind and body. It is often diffused or used topically in massages to alleviate stress, anxiety, and fatigue.

Mint oil in Africa is also valued for its mosquito repellent properties. The strong aroma of mint confuses mosquitoes and keeps them away. In regions where malaria is prevalent, mint oil is often applied to the body or clothes as a natural and safe alternative to chemical insect repellents.

Furthermore, mint oil has gained popularity in African skincare routines. Due to its antibacterial and antifungal properties, mint oil is used in various cosmetic products to combat acne, refresh the skin, and provide a cooling sensation. It is also effective in soothing insect bites, rashes, and skin irritation.

In conclusion, mint leaves and oil offer a multitude of uses and benefits in Africa. From their culinary applications to their medicinal properties and various other benefits, mint is a versatile herb that has enriched many aspects of African culture. Whether it is used in traditional dishes, for medicinal purposes, or in skincare and aromatherapy practices, mint leaves and oil have become an integral part of African heritage and continue to enhance the lives of many on the continent.

- The examples and recipes of cocktails using mint in Africa

Quench Your Thirst with African Mint Cocktails: A Delectable Journey of Refreshing Flavors

Mint, with its refreshing aroma and lively flavors, has been utilized in cocktails all over the world to create summer sensations. In this article, we will unravel the magnificent world of mint-infused cocktails brought to life by the diverse cultural tapestry of Africa. From North to South, East to West, the continent boasts a treasure trove of inspired recipes that skillfully combine local ingredients with the cooling essence of mint. Get ready to explore the rich heritage of African mixology and tantalize your taste buds with delightful cocktails that fuse tradition with innovation.

1. Moroccan Mojito:
Morocco's vibrant cocktail culture reflects the perfect blend of Mediterranean and North African flavors. The Moroccan Mojito is an irresistible fusion of classics, combining the zesty freshness of limes and mint with the unique sweetness of Moroccan honey. The traditional rum is artfully infused with refreshing mint leaves and bathed in fizzy soda water. Optional garnishes such as dried rose petals or citrus slices serve as a colorful finishing touch. This invigorating drink will transport you to the bustling streets of Marrakech in a single sip.

2. Rooibos Mint Julep:
South Africa's treasure, rooibos tea, inspires a delightful twist on the classic Mint Julep. Begin by steeping rooibos tea bags in bourbon, allowing the distinct flavor to infuse the spirit to perfection. Sugar is luxuriously dissolved into the brewed tea before adding an abundance of fresh mint leaves. Muddling the leaves releases their aromatic oils, resulting in an exquisite flavor blend that transforms the classic Julep. Served over crushed ice in a silver cup, adorned with sprigs of vibrant mint, this tipple is a celebration of

South African heritage.

3. Pomegranate and Mint Margarita:
North Africa offers a refreshingly exotic take on the beloved Margarita. This vibrant rendition boasts an enticing combination of tangy pomegranate juice and cooling mint, impeccably balanced with the classic trio of tequila, lime juice, and agave syrup. Fresh mint leaves are gently muddled with a muddler or the back of a spoon, releasing aromatic oils. Rimmed with a sprinkle of salt or sugar, this visually stunning cocktail delivers a taste of heightened sensational delight.

4. Gin and Moringa Mojito:
The vibrant tropics of West Africa introduce an intriguing blend of flavors in the Gin and Moringa Mojito. This cocktail showcases the unique properties of moringa leaves, brimming with health benefits and vibrant green color. In this enticing concoction, moringa leaves are incorporated directly into the cocktail, subtly enhancing the herbal notes of the gin. Combined with fresh mint leaves, lime juice, and a touch of sugar syrup, this truly distinctive cocktail showcases the wealth of nature found in West Africa.

The cocktails presented here provide just a glimpse into the treasure trove of African mixology that merges vibrant culture, local ingredients, and the refreshing essence of mint. Each region in Africa offers its own unique spin on traditional cocktails, adding a splash of character and revitalization to libations that are sure to delight the senses. Whether you find yourself in the sandy deserts of Morocco or amidst the lush rainforests of West Africa, you can now savor the storied traditions and exciting innovations of African mint cocktails wherever you may be. Embark on this flavor-filled journey and explore the diverse tastes that Africa has to offer in every sip.

Chapter 10: Cardamom - The Origin and Distribution of Cardamom in Africa

Cardamom, a highly aromatic spice known for its distinct flavor and therapeutic properties, has a rich history that spans continents and cultures. While it is commonly associated with Asian cuisine, particularly in India and Nepal, the origin and distribution of cardamom extend to other parts of the world as well. In this chapter, we will explore the fascinating journey of cardamom in Africa, uncovering its origins, historical significance, and current distribution across the continent.

The Origins of Cardamom in Africa:

The journey of cardamom in Africa traces back several centuries, with various historical accounts providing clues about its origin. Many believe that cardamom was introduced to Africa via ancient trade routes, linking the East African region to the Arabian Peninsula and the Indian subcontinent. Arab traders, who had extensive maritime networks, played a crucial role in spreading the cultivation and knowledge of cardamom across the region.

Distribution and Production of Cardamom in Africa:

Today, cardamom cultivation is primarily concentrated in a few countries in East Africa, namely Tanzania, Ethiopia, and Kenya. These countries have ideal climatic conditions and suitable soil types that support the growth and production of cardamom. Within Africa, Tanzania stands out as the largest producer of cardamom, accounting for a significant portion of total global production.

Tanzania:

Tanzania, located on the eastern coast of Africa, holds a prominent position in the cardamom industry. The southern regions of Tanzania, including the well-known spice-growing region of Tanga, have been at the forefront of cardamom cultivation in the country. The fertile soils and the tropical climate of Tanga create favorable conditions for the growth of both green and black cardamom varieties. Tanzanian cardamom is renowned for its robust flavor profile and high oil content, making it highly sought after in global markets.

Ethiopia:

Ethiopia, often referred to as the birthplace of coffee, also has a long history with cardamom cultivation. The southwestern part of the country, soaked in ancient trade routes, stands as a testament to the long-standing connection between Ethiopia and the spice. The Ethiopian variety of cardamom, known locally as Afar cardamom or Berebere cardamom, is highly prized for its unique taste and aroma. The highlands of Ethiopia offer optimal growing conditions, with altitudes ranging from 1,500 to 2,500 meters, contributing to the development of distinct flavor profiles in the spice.

Kenya:

While not as prominent as Tanzania and Ethiopia in terms of production scale, Kenya has been steadily expanding its cardamom cultivation. The coastal regions of Misieuni and Vanga have emerged as key areas for cardamom farming in the country. Here, farmers make use of the coastal climate, generous rainfall, and fertile soils to cultivate high-quality cardamom. Kenyan cardamom is treasured for its versatile usage, both as a flavoring agent and in traditional medicinal practices.

The Local Utilization and Influence of Cardamom in Africa:

Cardamom holds significant cultural and culinary importance across Africa. Locally, it is widely used in a variety of recipes ranging from curries, stews, beverages, and desserts, adding complexity and depth to the flavors. Furthermore, cardamom has been woven into the traditional African healing practices, where it is believed to possess medicinal properties such as digestive aid and relief for common ailments. The spice has seamlessly assimilated into the cultural fabric of various African communities, creating a unique fusion of cardamom-infused dishes.

The origin and distribution of cardamom in Africa can be traced back to historical trade routes and the influence of Arab traders. Today, Tanzania, Ethiopia, and Kenya serve as the primary hubs for cardamom cultivation in Africa, producing diverse and high-quality varieties. The utilization of cardamom in local cuisines and traditional healing practices further highlights the significance of this spice in African cultures. As both a testimony to ancient trade connections and a testament to the adaptability of cardamom across different continents, its presence in Africa continues to add depth and richness to the culinary heritage of the continent.

- The uses and benefits of cardamom pods and seeds in Africa

Cardamom, scientifically known as Elettaria cardamomum, is a spice that is widely used in African cuisine and traditional medicine. Native to the evergreen forests of the Western Ghats in India, this aromatic plant has made its way to various regions across Africa, where it has been recognized for its distinct flavor, medicinal properties, and numerous health benefits.

In African cuisine, cardamom seeds, pods, or powder are frequently added to recipes to enhance the taste and aroma of various dishes. Its unique flavor, combining hints of citrus, pine, and menthol, adds depth and complexity to a variety of meals, both savory and sweet. Often used in curry blends, stews, soups, and rice dishes, cardamom infuses a warm and slightly sweet undertone to these culinary creations.

Apart from being a popular culinary ingredient, cardamom also holds great significance in traditional African medicine. The seeds and pods of cardamom are believed to have many health benefits and therapeutic properties. Let's delve into some of the uses and benefits of cardamom in Africa:

1. Digestive Aid: Cardamom has long been used to aid digestion and relieve gastrointestinal discomfort. The essential oils present in the spice help to stimulate the production of digestive enzymes, improving digestion and reducing symptoms such as bloating, flatulence, and indigestion.

2. Oral Health: In certain African cultures, cardamom seeds function as a natural breath freshener and oral health remedy. Chewing on cardamom pods can help combat bad breath, as its antibacterial properties help eliminate odor-causing bacteria in the mouth. Additionally, cardamom is used in traditional remedies to alleviate toothaches and gum infections.

3. Respiratory Health: The aromatic compounds found in cardamom have been prized in traditional African medicine for their beneficial effects on the respiratory system. Boiling cardamom pods and inhaling the steam is commonly practiced to clear blocked sinuses, ease coughs, and relieve symptoms of colds and respiratory infections.

4. Anti-inflammatory and Antioxidant Properties: Cardamom is rich in antioxidants, which help neutralize harmful free radicals in the body, reducing inflammation and oxidative stress. These properties may protect against chronic diseases, such as heart disease, cancer, and age-related cognitive decline.

5. Diuretic Effects: Traditionally, cardamom has been used as a diuretic, promoting urination and aiding in the removal of excess water and toxins from the body. This makes it valuable in managing conditions such as kidney stones, urinary tract infections, and edema.

6. Aphrodisiac Properties: Cardamom has been coveted for its alleged aphrodisiac properties in various African cultures. It is believed to enhance virility and sexual desire. Additionally, cardamom's exotic aroma is often associated with luxury and sensuality, further contributing to its reputation as an aphrodisiac spice.

Given the various health benefits and culinary uses of cardamom, it comes as no surprise that this aromatic spice holds a prominent place in African cuisine and traditional medicine. Whether it's adding depth to a savory dish or offering relief from various ailments, cardamom pods and seeds serve as an invaluable resource for enhancing both culinary experiences and overall well-being throughout Africa.

- The examples and recipes of cocktails using cardamom in Africa

In Africa, particularly in countries like Ethiopia, Somalia, and Libya, cardamom is a popular spice used in a variety of culinary preparations and beverages. Its distinct aroma and warm, citrusy flavor add a unique touch to any dish or drink. When it comes to incorporating cardamom into cocktails, the possibilities are truly endless. From classic favorites to unique concoctions, here are some examples and recipes of cocktails using cardamom in Africa.

1. Ethiopian Spiced Martini:
This delightful twist on a classic martini celebrates the rich flavors of Ethiopia. To make this cocktail, muddle 1 green cardamom pod with a teaspoon of sugar and a dash of orange bitters. Add 2 ounces of vodka and shake with ice. Strain into a chilled martini glass and garnish with a lemon twist.

2. Somali Safari Sour:
Transport yourself to the vibrant plains of Somalia with this refreshing whiskey-based cocktail. Begin by muddling 2 green cardamom pods with a piece of fresh ginger and a teaspoon of honey. Add 2 ounces of whiskey, the juice of half a lemon, and a dash of cinnamon. Shake vigorously with ice and strain into a rocks glass filled with fresh ice. Garnish with a slice of lemon.

3. Karkadeh and Cardamom Breeze:

Utilizing the tangy flavors of hibiscus, this Egyptian-inspired cocktail will invigorate your taste buds. Start by steeping 2 teaspoons of dried hibiscus flowers and 2 crushed cardamom pods in 6 ounces of boiling water. Let it cool and strain into a pitcher. Add 1 ounce of gin, a squeeze of lime juice, a splash of soda water, and ice cubes. Stir well and serve in a tall glass garnished with a lime wheel.

4. Cape Malay Colada:
This tropical South African twist on the classic piña colada will transport you to the sunny shores of Cape Town. In a blender, combine 1 cup of pineapple chunks, 2 ounces of rum, 1 ounce of coconut cream, 1 teaspoon of crushed green cardamom pods, and a squeeze of lime juice. Blend until smooth, pour into a tall glass, and garnish with a pineapple wedge and a sprinkle of ground cardamom.

5. Tunisian Date Night:
Indulge in the sweet and aromatic flavors of Tunisia with this enticing cocktail. In a shaker, muddle 2 Medjool dates with 1 teaspoon of honey, the juice of half an orange, and the seeds from 1 green cardamom pod. Add 2 ounces of vodka and shake well with ice. Strain into a chilled martini glass and garnish with an orange twist.

These examples and recipes are just a glimpse into the wonderful world of cardamom-infused cocktails in Africa. Whether you're looking for a traditional flavor or a unique twist, incorporating cardamom into your cocktails will surely elevate your drinking experience with its exotic charm. Cheers!

Chapter 11: Cinnamon - The Origin and Distribution of Cinnamon in Africa

Cinnamon, a fragrant and versatile spice, has captivated the taste buds of people all around the world for centuries. While commonly associated with Southeast Asia and the Middle East, the origin and distribution of cinnamon have fascinating roots that stretch back to the African continent. In this chapter, we will delve deep into the realm of cinnamon and explore its journey and significance in Africa.

Historical Background

Cinnamon, scientifically known as Cinnamomum, is derived from the inner bark of tree species belonging to the Lauraceae family. The use of cinnamon dates back thousands of years and has been documented in ancient texts and manuscripts. The ancient Egyptians were known to employ the spice in their embalming process, while during the Roman Empire, cinnamon was considered a luxurious and highly valued commodity.

Origins in Africa

Contrary to popular belief, cinnamon did not originate in Asia but in fact, was first discovered on the African continent. The precise origin of cinnamon is often associated with the ancient kingdom of Ethiopia, present-day Ethiopia and Eritrea. The historic Ethiopian trade routes traversed through the Red Sea to India, providing travelers and traders with access to this prized spice. Subsequently, cinnamon made its way across the Mediterranean, transforming into a coveted and sought-after spice in the Western world.

Distribution across Africa

Apart from its origin, cinnamon has also flourished and diversified its distribution across various regions of Africa. The colonial era significantly influenced the spread of cinnamon plantations throughout the continent. African countries such as Madagascar, Tanzania, and Zanzibar became major contributors to the global cinnamon market with their fertile lands and optimum climatic conditions. To meet the growing demand for the spice, cinnamon plantations were established, and the farming practices were refined and improved over time.

Madagascar is recognized as a significant producer of cinnamon, and it boasts a unique variety, known as Madagascar or Bourbon cinnamon. The lush forests of the island nation provide an ideal habitat for cinnamon trees, resulting in high-quality cinnamon with rich flavor profiles. The production of cinnamon not only presents economic benefits for Madagascar but also contributes to the preservation of its diverse ecosystem.

Tanzania and Zanzibar, situated along the eastern coast of Africa, have also cultivated a thriving cinnamon industry. The cinnamon trees thrive in the fertile soils and warm tropical climate of the region. These African countries have achieved commendable success in cinnamon production, gaining recognition in worldwide markets.

Significance and Culinary Uses

Cinnamon is not merely a spice; it holds immense cultural, medicinal, and culinary significance in Africa. Its versatile and aromatic nature adds a delightful touch to both sweet and savory dishes across various African cuisines. In traditional African medicine, cinnamon is believed to possess healing properties, benefiting ailments such as colds, digestive issues, and infections. Furthermore, cinnamon is used in traditional African rituals and ceremonies due to its association with prosperity and abundance.

Conclusion

As we conclude our exploration of cinnamon's origin and distribution in Africa, it is clear that the continent plays a significant role in the global cinnamon industry. From its early discovery in Ethiopia to the successful plantations in Madagascar, Tanzania, and Zanzibar, Africa's contribution to the cultivation and distribution of cinnamon cannot be overlooked. The flavorful cinnamon varieties produced in African countries enrich the culinary experiences of people worldwide while leaving a lasting impact on their socio-economic development.

- The uses and benefits of cinnamon bark and powder in Africa

Cinnamon is a well-known spice that is widely used in various culinary dishes and beverages across the globe. While it is popularly associated with countries like Sri Lanka and India, cinnamon bark and powder also have rich uses and benefits in Africa. In this article, we will explore the various ways cinnamon is utilized in the African continent and highlight its numerous health benefits.

Cinnamon, scientifically known as Cinnamomum verum, possesses a distinct flavor and aroma that can enhance the taste of any dish. In Africa, cinnamon finds application in both traditional and modern cuisine. It is not uncommon to find cinnamon being used as a key ingredient in stews, soups, marinades, and desserts. Often, it is blended with other spices like nutmeg, cloves, and ginger to create unique flavor profiles.

One prominent example of cinnamon usage in African cuisine is found in Morocco's rich culinary heritage. Moroccan cuisine often includes the sweet and warm taste of cinnamon in dishes like tagines and couscous. The spice adds a delicious aroma and depth of flavor to these traditional meals.

Moreover, cinnamon is celebrated for its medicinal properties across Africa. In traditional African medicine, the bark and powder of cinnamon are utilized for their various health benefits. Chiefs, healers, and traditional medicine practitioners have long relied on cinnamon for its anti-inflammatory, antimicrobial, and analgesic properties.

Cinnamon is also recognized for its ability to aid digestion. In many African cultures, it is often consumed after meals as a digestive aid or added to herbal teas for a soothing effect on the stomach. Furthermore, cinnamon promotes appetite and relieves flatulence in many individuals.

Another notable use of cinnamon in Africa lies in its potential to manage blood sugar levels. Several studies have suggested that cinnamon can improve insulin sensitivity and help regulate blood glucose levels, making it a valuable tool in the management of diabetes. In countries like Ghana and Nigeria, cinnamon is often used in traditional medicine to support diabetes treatment.

In addition to its medicinal benefits, cinnamon is employed for various non-culinary purposes as well. In several African nations, cinnamon oil is extracted from the bark and powders and used in the production of perfumes and cosmetics. The warm and sweet aroma of cinnamon adds a distinct note to various beauty products, contributing to their popularity and demand.

Furthermore, cinnamon's preserved bark acts as a natural insect repellent. In regions where insects are a nuisance, cinnamon sticks are strategically placed to deter these pests from entering homes and food storage areas. Unlike harmful chemical repellents, cinnamon offers a natural solution that is safe for humans and the environment.

In conclusion, cinnamon bark and powder hold immense importance and benefit in Africa. Whether it is used in traditional cuisine, traditional medicine, as a fragrance enhancer, or as an insect repellent, cinnamon's versatile characteristics make it an integral part of African culture and everyday life. Furthermore, scientists and researchers continue to explore cinnamon's many health benefits, elevating its status as a valuable spice with significant medicinal value.

- The examples and recipes of cocktails using cinnamon in Africa

Africa is brimming with vibrant flavors and spices, and one such spice that adds that aromatic touch to cocktails is cinnamon. Known for its warm, earthy and slightly sweet aroma, cinnamon has been a beloved addition in African cuisine for centuries. Today, we will explore some tantalizing examples and recipes of cocktails that utilize the enchanting essence of cinnamon.

1. African Spiced Mojito:
Start by muddling fresh mint leaves, a pinch of ground cinnamon, and a spoonful of brown sugar in a cocktail shaker. Add the juice of one lime and two ounces of white rum. Shake well and strain the mixture into a glass filled with ice. Top it off with a splash of sparkling water and garnish with a cinnamon stick and a sprig of fresh mint.

2. Cape Town Cinnamon Glühwein:
This is a delightful beverage that adds a splash of warmth to cozy evenings. In a pot, combine two cups of red wine, two cinnamon sticks, six cloves, orange peel, and a few slices of fresh ginger. Heat the mixture gently without boiling, allowing the flavors to infuse for about 30 minutes. Add two tablespoons of honey or brown sugar for a touch of sweetness. Strain the spiced concoction into heatproof glasses and garnish with a cinnamon stick or an orange wedge.

3. Moroccan Chai Martini:
For a sophisticated twist on the classic martini, prepare a cup of strongly brewed Rooibos tea and let it cool. In a cocktail shaker, combine two ounces of vodka, three ounces of cooled Rooibos tea, one ounce of honey syrup (equal parts honey and hot water mixed together), and a hint of ground cinnamon. Shake vigorously until well mixed, then strain into a martini glass. Garnish with a sprinkle of ground cinnamon or a cinnamon stick.

4. Sudanese Cinnamon Sour:
To create this citrusy and spiced cocktail, start by mixing two ounces of bourbon, one ounce of fresh lemon juice, half an ounce of simple syrup, and a pinch of ground cinnamon in a shaker filled with ice. Shake well. Strain the mixture into a rocks glass filled with ice and garnish with a cinnamon stick or a lemon twist.

5. Tanzanian Cinnamon Coffee Cocktail:
For coffee lovers, this recipe provides a delightful twist. Begin by brewing a cup of strong coffee and letting it cool. In a mixing glass, combine two ounces of Tanzanian coffee liqueur, one ounce of vodka, and half an ounce of cinnamon syrup (simmer equal parts water, sugar, and cinnamon sticks until well dissolved, then let it cool). Stir well to mix the ingredients. Pour the mixture into a tall glass filled with ice and carefully add the cooled coffee. Garnish with a sprinkle of ground cinnamon or a cinnamon stick for an added visual appeal.

These examples and recipes reflect the creative fusion of traditional African ingredients with cinnamon, resulting in exciting and aromatic cocktails. Whether you prefer them sweet, spicy, or a combination of both, exploring the world of cinnamon-infused cocktails will surely take your taste buds on an exquisite African journey.

Chapter 12: Nutmeg - The Origin and Distribution of Nutmeg in Africa

Nutmeg is a well-known spice derived from the seeds of the Myristica fragrance tree. Although native to the Maluku Islands in Indonesia, nutmeg has been cultivated and traded across the globe for centuries. Africa, often the focus of discussions on its vast biodiversity, also holds a vital role in nutmeg production. In this chapter, we will unravel the fascinating origin and distribution of nutmeg in Africa, shedding light on the economies and cultures linked with this aromatic spice.

1. Historical Background:

The story of African nutmeg begins with the Portuguese explorer and navigator Vasco Da Gama, who reached the East African coast in the late 15th century. Da Gama's discovery initiated the establishment of numerous trade routes, connecting Africa with major spice-producing regions. During this period, Arab traders introduced nutmeg in Africa, stirring interest in its cultivation and usage.

2. Climate and Soil Requirements:

Nutmeg trees thrive in tropical climates with adequate rainfall and temperatures that average between 20°C-30°C (68°F-86°F). African countries such as Tanzania, Madagascar, and Nigeria provide the ideal conditions for nutmeg cultivation. Well-drained volcanic soils rich in organic matter are particularly suitable for the growth of these trees.

3. Distribution:

a) Madagascar:

Madagascar, located off the southeastern coast of Africa, is renowned for its diverse species of flora and fauna. The fertile soil and favorable climate make it an exceptional nutmeg-growing region. Mainly concentrated in the northeast and northwest parts of the country, nutmeg plantations flourish amidst lush rainforests. Madagascar has gained recognition as one of the largest nutmeg exporters in Africa.

b) Tanzania:

Nutmeg production in Tanzania has a rich history dating back to the colonial era. Zanzibar, an island archipelago along Tanzania's eastern coast, was a significant hub for nutmeg cultivation under the control of the Sultan of Oman. Today, the islands of Pemba and Zanzibar still harbor vast nutmeg plantations, maintaining Tanzania's prominence in the African nutmeg trade.

c) Nigeria:

Originating from seedlings brought by Portuguese traders, nutmeg cultivation in Nigeria gained traction during the 19th century. Nigeria's fertile lands, particularly in the south, provide favorable conditions for nutmeg tree cultivation. The country has fostered a thriving domestic nutmeg industry, with exports reaching various African and international markets.

4. Economic Significance:

The cultivation of nutmeg plays a significant role in the economies of Madagascar, Tanzania, and Nigeria. The trade of nutmeg contributes to agricultural development, foreign exchange earnings, and employment opportunities in these countries. Additionally, it stimulates rural development by creating a market for small-scale farmers, increasing export revenues, and improving the standard of living for many communities.

5. Cultural Significance:

Nutmeg holds cultural significance in several African societies. Often used as a cooking spice, it adds depth and aroma to traditional dishes such as curries, stews, and sweets. Additionally, nutmeg is an important ingredient in certain traditional medicines, believed to possess aphrodisiac and healing properties.

6. Challenges and Future Prospects:

Despite the promising prospects for nutmeg cultivation in Africa, challenges remain. Limited modern farming techniques, inadequate infrastructure, and climate change pose significant threats to its successful production. However, with increased investments in research, improved agricultural practices, and enhanced trade networks, the African nutmeg industry can thrive, contributing further to economic growth and sustainable livelihoods.

The origin and distribution of nutmeg in Africa unveil a captivating narrative encompassing trade, colonization, agriculture, and cultural practices. African countries like Madagascar, Tanzania, and Nigeria have successfully integrated nutmeg production into their agricultural landscapes, granting economic benefits and emphasizing the importance of this aromatic spice in their respective cultures. By addressing challenges and nurturing the potential for growth, Africa's nutmeg industry remains poised to make substantial contributions to global spice markets in the coming years.

- The uses and benefits of nutmeg seeds and powder in Africa

Nutmeg, an aromatic spice derived from the seeds of Myristica fragrans, is widely known for its culinary uses in various cuisines around the world. However, its benefits and uses go beyond just adding flavor to dishes. In Africa, nutmeg seeds and powder are employed in traditional medicine, religious ceremonies, and even for cosmetic purposes.

In traditional medicine, nutmeg is highly regarded for its medicinal properties. It is often used as a natural remedy for various ailments, thanks to its numerous active compounds. The seeds of nutmeg are packed with antioxidants, vitamins, and minerals, making them a valuable addition to traditional healing practices.

One of the most well-known uses of nutmeg in Africa is its ability to alleviate gastrointestinal problems. The spice is believed to aid in digestion, reduce flatulence, relieve bloating, and alleviate stomachaches. Nutmeg powder is often mixed with other herbal ingredients to create medicinal teas or infusions that help soothe the digestive system.

Additionally, nutmeg is known for its analgesic properties, making it a popular choice for alleviating pain and inflammation. In traditional medicine, nutmeg can be crushed into a paste and applied topically to painful joints, sore muscles, or even toothaches. It is believed to provide temporary pain relief and reduce inflammation due to its active ingredient called myristicin.

Moreover, nutmeg has calming effects on the nervous system, making it beneficial for individuals suffering from mental health issues such as anxiety, depression, or insomnia. In Africa, it is not uncommon to find nutmeg being used as a natural sedative or anti-depressant. Nutmeg powder is often combined with other herbs or spices to create medicinal concoctions that promote better sleep and overall mental well-being.

In certain African cultures, nutmeg also plays a significant role in religious ceremonies and rituals. It is considered to have spiritual properties, believed to cleanse and purify the mind, body, and soul. The seeds or powder are sometimes burned as incense during spiritual practices, invoking a sense of tranquility and spiritual connection.

Furthermore, nutmeg has been incorporated into cosmetic products in Africa for centuries. It is known for its skin-healing properties and is often used to treat acne, scars, and other skin conditions. Nutmeg powder can be mixed with honey, yogurt, or various natural oils to create face masks or scrubs that nourish the skin, reduce inflammation, and promote a healthy complexion.

In conclusion, nutmeg seeds and powder offer a wide range of uses and benefits in Africa. Whether it is utilized in traditional medicine, religious ceremonies, or as a cosmetic ingredient, nutmeg's medicinal properties make it a valuable resource. From soothing gastrointestinal issues to improving mental well-being, nutmeg plays a significant role in enhancing the overall health and vitality of individuals in Africa.

- The examples and recipes of cocktails using nutmeg in Africa

Nutmeg-Based Cocktail Delights from Africa: Examples and Recipes

From its origins in Southeast Asia, nutmeg has made its way to numerous continents, including Africa. The addition of nutmeg to cocktails brings a unique and tantalizing element, enhancing the flavors and providing an exotic twist. In this article, we delve into the fascinating world of nutmeg-infused cocktails found across different regions of Africa, exploring various examples and recipes guaranteed to captivate your taste buds.

1. East African Delight: Spiced Zanzibar Cocktail
The spice-rich island of Zanzibar is known for its vibrant flavors, and the Spiced Zanzibar Cocktail embodies this reputation perfectly. Blending African spices, including nutmeg, with tropical fruits, this cocktail tantalizes your senses with its enticing aroma and refreshing taste. To create this concoction, combine 2 ounces of rum, 1 ounce of pineapple juice, ½ fresh lime juice, ¼ ounce of simple syrup, and a pinch of freshly grated nutmeg. Shake well with ice and strain into a chilled cocktail glass. Garnish with a pineapple wedge and sprinkle some grated nutmeg on top for an authentic African touch.

2. West African Twist: Nigerian Chapman

The jovial Nigerian Chapman is a beloved drink popular in West Africa, often served at social gatherings and celebrations. Combining fruit juices, aromatic bitters, and a sprinkle of nutmeg, this colorful cocktail strikes a perfect balance between sweet, sour, and bitter notes. To prepare a Nigerian Chapman, combine 10 ounces of Fanta Orange or Sprite, 2 ounces of Angostura bitters, 1 ounce of grenadine syrup, and the juice of one lime in a pitcher. Stir well to mix the flavors thoroughly. Serve in highball glasses filled with ice cubes, garnished with orange slices and a light sprinkling of nutmeg.

3. Central African Elixir: African Sunset

The enchanting African Sunset cocktail pays homage to Central Africa's captivating beauty and rich cultural diversity. Blending aromatic spices like nutmeg with tangy citrus flavors, this delightful cocktail captures the essence of the region marvelously. Begin by combining 1.5 ounces of vodka, 1 ounce of passion fruit juice, ½ ounce of fresh lemon juice, and ¼ ounce of grenadine syrup in a shaker filled with ice. Shake vigorously, then strain into a chilled coupe glass. Sprinkle a pinch of freshly grated nutmeg on top for an intriguing finishing touch.

4. North African Refresher: Moroccan Mule

Immerse yourself in the aromatic flavors of North Africa with the beloved Moroccan Mule. Infusing traditional Moroccan spices, including nutmeg, into a classic Mule cocktail, this refreshing concoction embodies the essence of Moroccan hospitality. To create a Moroccan Mule, combine 1.5 ounces of vodka, ½ ounce of freshly squeezed lime juice, 2 dashes of Angostura bitters, and a few sprigs of fresh mint in a copper Moscow Mule mug filled with ice. Top with ginger beer and stir gently. Grate a little nutmeg on top, garnish with a lime wedge, and enjoy the enticing blend of exotic flavors.

Africa's diverse cuisines and cultures have enriched the world of mixology with an array of captivating nutmeg-infused cocktails. These examples have provided a glimpse into the fascinating range of flavors and preparations found throughout the continent. Embark upon a sensory adventure by exploring the distinctive recipes of nutmeg-based cocktails from East, West,

Central, and North Africa, and let the magic of this enchanting spice forge an everlasting connection between your taste buds and the rich heritage of the African continent.

Chapter 13: Clove – The origin and distribution of clove in Africa

Originating from the Maluku Islands in Indonesia, cloves have traversed the seas to reach several regions of Africa. Their distinct flavor and medicinal properties have endeared them to various cultures across the continent. In this chapter, we delve into the fascinating story of clove's journey to Africa and its current distribution on the continent.

Clove's journey to Africa began in the 13th century when Arab traders introduced this valuable spice to the East African coast. Zanzibar, in particular, emerged as a pivotal hub for the spice trade, with its lush green valleys and tropical climate providing the perfect environment for clove cultivation. Under the Sultanate of Oman's rule in the 18th century, Zanzibar claimed its fame as the "Spice Island," thriving on the production and export of cloves.

The suitable climatic conditions of Zanzibar attracted cloves to take root and thrive in this pristine region. The ideal combination of rainfall, humidity, and rich volcanic soil yields aromatic, high-quality cloves that are the envy of spice connoisseurs worldwide. The locals soon realized the lucrative potential of clove production, leading to the establishment of vast plantations across the archipelago.

The booming clove industry in Zanzibar also drew attention from other countries in East Africa, leading to the expansion of plantations in regions such as Pemba Island, Tanzania, and Kenya. Clove trees, scientifically known as Syzygium aromaticum, found a fertile home in these areas, mimicking the ideal conditions of their native land.

Beyond East Africa, clove also found its way to other parts of the continent. Communities in Madagascar cultivated cloves, contributing to the spice's distribution in the Indian Ocean region. The African Great Lakes region, including countries such as Rwanda, Uganda, and Burundi, witnessed the introduction of clove farming, albeit on a smaller scale. While cloves faced challenges adapting to the different climatic conditions in these regions, small-scale plantations sprang up, meeting local demand for the prized spice.

With rich soil, a unique microclimate, and dedicated farmers, Africa has firmly established itself as a player in the global clove market. Today, Zanzibar remains the largest producer and exporter of the spice in Africa, accounting for a significant portion of the world's clove trade. Other regions on the continent, including Madagascar, Tanzania, and Kenya, continue to contribute to Africa's growing clove industry.

The distribution of clove plantations is often concentrated around coastal areas due to the beneficial marine influence, which ensures a constant temperature range for optimum growth. Inland regions cannot afford the luxury of these climatic conditions, making coastal areas the primary focus for clove production.

As these regions become internationally recognized for their superior cloves, they embrace the responsibility of upholding the quality and reputation of African-grown clove. This entails adopting sustainable farming practices, efficient processing techniques, and stringent quality control measures. To maintain a competitive edge in the global market, these regions continually strive to improve agricultural techniques and invest in research and development.

The journey of cloves to Africa has had a profound impact on the continent's history, culture, and economy. From its humble beginnings in the Maluku Islands to becoming a vital component of African spice trade, cloves exemplify the power of cross-cultural exchange and globalization. Today, they are not only an integral part of African cuisine but also widely used in traditional medicine, fragrances, and even dental care products.

In conclusion, clove's origin and distribution in Africa tell a compelling story of human ingenuity, historical trade routes, and the adaptability of a precious botanical resource. With the continent's diverse climates and favorable growing conditions, Africa's production and distribution of cloves contribute significantly to the spice's global trade. As the demand for this culinary treasure continues to rise, one can only anticipate the increasing importance of African cloves in the future.

- The uses and benefits of clove buds and oil in Africa

Clove buds and oil have a long history of traditional uses in Africa, where they are valued for their various benefits. These small, aromatic flower buds from the Syzygium aromaticum tree, native to the Maluku Islands in Indonesia, have made their way to Africa through trade routes and have become an integral part of the continent's traditional medicine and cuisine. In this article, we will explore the uses and benefits of clove buds and oil in Africa.

1. Oral Health:
Clove buds and oil have been used for centuries in Africa to promote oral health. Due to their powerful antibacterial and analgesic properties, they are often used to treat toothaches, mouth sores, and gum infections. Many traditional African communities also use clove oil as an ingredient in their mouthwashes and toothpaste to maintain oral hygiene.

2. Digestive Aid:
In African culinary traditions, clove buds and oil are valued for their ability to aid digestion. This spice is often added to dishes to improve nutrient absorption, ease bloating and gas, and relieve indigestion. Moreover, clove oil can alleviate gastrointestinal issues such as constipation and stomach ulcers when used in appropriate amounts.

3. Antimicrobial Properties:
Clove buds and oil possess potent antimicrobial properties, which are particularly useful in a continent where various infectious diseases are prevalent. Traditional healers often use clove-based remedies to treat conditions caused by bacteria or fungi. Clove oil can be applied topically to wounds, skin infections, or fungal conditions like athlete's foot to inhibit the

growth of microorganisms.

4. Pain Relief:
Clove buds and oil have analgesic properties thanks to their high concentration of eugenol, a compound known for its pain-relieving effects. In many African countries, clove oil is used topically to alleviate pain from conditions like headaches, arthritis, muscle stiffness, and even minor injuries.

5. Respiratory Conditions:
Clove buds and oil are commonly used in Africa to relieve symptoms of respiratory ailments like coughs, asthma, and bronchitis. The oil can be inhaled through steam or applied topically on the chest to facilitate easier breathing, open up congested airways, and help to clear phlegm.

6. Insect Repellent:
In regions where mosquito-borne diseases such as malaria are prevalent, clove oil is often used as a natural insect repellent. Applied to exposed skin or mixed into lotions and creams, it acts as a barrier against mosquitoes, ticks, and other biting insects, thus reducing the risk of acquiring such diseases.

7. Culinary Uses:
Last but not least, clove buds and oil are widely used in African cuisines to enhance flavors and add aroma. They are a key ingredient in spice blends like Ethiopian berbere and North African ras el hanout. Cloves are used to season dishes such as stews, soups, rice, meats, and desserts, giving them a distinct, warm, and slightly sweet flavor.

In conclusion, clove buds and oil have a wide range of uses and benefits in Africa. From promoting oral health to providing pain relief, aiding digestion, and acting as a natural insect repellent, their versatility and medicinal properties have made them indispensable in traditional African medicine and culinary practices. As a result, clove buds and oil continue to play a crucial role in the daily lives and well-being of many people across the continent.

- The examples and recipes of cocktails using clove in Africa

In Africa, cloves have been used for centuries not only for their aromatic and flavorful properties but also for their medicinal benefits. The intense and warming taste of cloves adds a unique twist to a variety of cocktails, creating an exotic and complex flavor profile. Let's explore some fascinating examples and recipes of cocktails using cloves in Africa.

1. Zanzibar Spice Martini:
Zanzibar, a picturesque island off the coast of Tanzania, is famous for its spice plantations, including cloves. The Zanzibar Spice Martini is a vibrant and spicy cocktail that captures the essence of this fascinating place.

Ingredients:
- 2 ounces of spiced rum
- 1 ounce of freshly squeezed lime juice
- 1/2 ounce of simple syrup
- 2 whole cloves
- Ice cubes

Instructions:
1. In a mixing glass, muddle the cloves with simple syrup to release their flavor.
2. Add the spiced rum and lime juice to the mixing glass.
3. Fill the glass with ice cubes and stir well to chill the mixture.
4. Place a fine strainer over your martini glass and strain the cocktail into it.
5. Garnish with a lime twist or a clove-studded lime wheel for decoration.

2. Cape Mulled Wine:
Mulling wine with spices is a popular practice in South Africa, especially during the cooler months. The Cape Mulled Wine combines the warmth of red wine with the comforting aroma of cloves and other spices.

Ingredients:
- 1 bottle of red wine (such as Shiraz or Merlot)
- 4 cups of apple cider or cranberry juice
- 1/4 cup of honey or brown sugar
- 1 orange, sliced
- 10 cloves
- 4 cinnamon sticks
- 2 star anise pods

Instructions:
1. Pour the red wine and the apple cider or cranberry juice into a large pot.
2. Add the honey or brown sugar, orange slices, cloves, cinnamon sticks, and star anise pods.
3. Place the pot over low heat and slowly warm the mixture, but avoid boiling it.
4. Let the flavors infuse for at least 20 minutes, but longer if desired.
5. Ladle the mulled wine into mugs, making sure to include some of the aromatic spices.
6. Enjoy this cozy African delight by garnishing each mug with a cinnamon stick or orange slice.

3. Moroccan Clove Mojito:
In North Africa, including Morocco, mint tea is an integral part of culture. Infusing the refreshing flavors of mint and cloves into a classic mojito creates a captivating Moroccan Clove Mojito.

Ingredients:
- 8 fresh mint leaves
- Juice of 1 lime
- 2 teaspoons of sugar
- 2 whole cloves
- 2 ounces of white rum
- Club soda
- Ice cubes

Instructions:
1. In a tall glass, muddle the mint leaves with lime juice, sugar, and cloves to

release the flavors.
2. Fill the glass halfway with ice cubes.
3. Pour the white rum over the ice and stir well.
4. Top the glass with club soda.
5. Garnish with a sprig of fresh mint and a clove-speared lime wedge.

These delightful examples and recipes of cocktails using cloves in Africa showcase the versatility and rich cultural background of this unique spice. Whether you are enjoying a Zanzibar Spice Martini, sipping on a Cape Mulled Wine, or indulging in a Moroccan Clove Mojito, you are sure to embark on a tantalizing journey fueled by the taste and aroma of cloves.

Chapter 14: Vanilla- The Origin and Distribution of Vanilla in Africa

Vanilla, popularly known for its rich aroma and flavor, is one of the most sought-after spices in the world today. Although it is widely known as a flavoring agent in baking and cooking, few people are aware of its fascinating origin and distribution. This chapter aims to explore the history and origin of vanilla specifically in Africa, shedding light on its intriguing journey across the continent.

1. The Origins of Vanilla:
The story of vanilla traces back to ancient Mesoamerica, specifically in present-day Mexico and Central America. However, its journey towards Africa is said to have begun during the era of colonialization and bustling transcontinental trade.

2. Exploration and Introduction to Africa:
The Portuguese, French, and Dutch explorers ventured through the Indian Ocean in search of new trade routes and exotic goods. These seafarers encountered vanilla on their expeditions, discovering its unique flavoring and aromatic properties. Being astute businessmen, they realized the potential in bringing this remarkable spice to various parts of the world, including Africa.

3. Zanzibar- The Vanilla Hub:
The island of Zanzibar, located off the eastern coast of Africa, played a crucial role in the distribution of vanilla throughout the continent. This tropical paradise emerged as a flourishing trading center, primarily due to its proximity to the mainland and suitable climate for vanilla cultivation.

4. Vanilla in East Africa:
Initially, vanilla was introduced to East Africa, specifically in countries like Tanzania, Madagascar, and the Comoros Islands. The humid climate and

fertile soil of these regions provided ideal conditions for growing this temperamental orchid vine.

5. Vanilla Adaptation:
As vanilla started to be cultivated in Africa, it adapted to the local environment, leading to the development of distinct varieties. This evolution resulted in unique flavor profiles, distinguishing African vanilla from its counterparts in other regions.

6. The Birth of Madagascar Vanilla:
The island of Madagascar eventually became the prime producer of vanilla in Africa due to its favorable climate and rich volcanic soil. This distinctive region yielded outstanding vanilla beans known for their exceptional quality and flavors that became highly revered worldwide.

7. The Global Trade Impact:
During the 19th and 20th centuries, African vanilla, especially the sought-after Madagascar vanilla, made a significant impact on the world's vanilla trade. Its popularity surged, leading to increased demand from renowned culinary cultures and industries worldwide.

8. Challenges and Conservation Efforts:
The vanilla industry in Africa faced various challenges over the years, including climatic fluctuations, pests, diseases, and price fluctuations. Nevertheless, efforts have been undertaken to advocate for sustainable vanilla production, educating farmers on cultivation techniques, and preserving the elusive vanilla orchid species for future generations.

The origin and distribution of vanilla in Africa reveal a captivating tale of exploration, trade, and ingenuity. Vanilla's journey from Mesoamerica to its adaptation and cultivation in Africa created a rich tapestry of flavor and aroma, ultimately influencing global culinary traditions. Despite the challenges faced, African vanilla remains a prized commodity, cherished for its unique characteristics and valuable contribution to the spice industry.

- The uses and benefits of vanilla beans and extract in Africa

The Wonders of Vanilla: Unveiling Its Uses and Benefits in Africa

Vanilla is a globally adored flavor, famous for its sweet aromatic quality that enhances a myriad of delicacies. Although it has its roots in Mesoamerican regions, vanilla has found its way to various corners of the world, including Africa, where it thrives today. In this article, we will explore the numerous uses and benefits of vanilla beans and extract in Africa, shedding light on its impact on local communities, culinary traditions, and even the economy.

1. Culinary Delights:
- Vanilla as a Flavor Enhancer: Vanilla extract is extensively used in African cuisines, imparting a delicious, distinctive flavor to various dishes, both sweet and savory. From rice puddings to vegetable curries, vanilla enhances the overall taste and takes dishes to a new level.
- Baked Goods and Pastries: Vanilla extract brings warmth and depth to cakes, cookies, and pastries. Be it the delicate African sponge cake or traditional pastries such as mandazi, by adding vanilla, bakers create mouthwatering treats adored by locals and tourists alike.
- Traditional African Drinks: African beverages have their own unique flavors, and vanilla plays a crucial role in complementing and enriching them. For instance, vanilla is used in vanilla-infused tea or spices up delicious beverages like bissap in Senegal or "madafu"- young coconut water infused with vanilla in Tanzania.

2. Health Benefits:
- Anti-Inflammatory Properties: Vanillin, the primary organic compound found in vanilla beans, possesses anti-inflammatory properties, which can be beneficial in easing inflammation-related ailments like arthritis and promoting general joint health.
- Antioxidant-rich: Vanilla is abundant in antioxidants, which can help fight

against harmful free radicals in the body. These antioxidants provide a range of benefits, such as enhancing the immune system, reducing oxidative stress, and lowering the risk of chronic diseases like cancer and heart disease.
- Stress-relieving properties: The use of vanilla-scented candles or even sipping a cup of vanilla-infused tea is thought to have a calming effect, as the aroma stimulates the release of mood-enhancing endorphins, promoting relaxation and reducing stress and anxiety.

3. Beauty and Aromatherapy:
- Aromatherapy: Vanilla possesses soothing and comforting notes, making it a popular choice in aromatherapy for creating a relaxing atmosphere. Diffusing vanilla-scented oils or using vanilla-infused bath products helps to relieve stress, anxiety, and sleep disorders.
- Skincare: Vanilla's antioxidant properties make it beneficial for skin health. When added to skincare products, it can help protect the skin from damage caused by free radicals, leading to healthier, rejuvenated skin.

4. Economic Impact:
- Income Generation for Farmers: Vanilla farming provides a stable source of income for many small-scale farmers in Africa, particularly in countries like Madagascar, Uganda and Comoros. These regions produce a significant portion of the world's vanilla beans, contributing to job creation and poverty alleviation.
- Export Opportunities: The demand for high-quality African vanilla is growing globally, presenting Africa with valuable export opportunities. This enables increased international trade, thereby boosting the local economy and fostering economic development.

The uses and benefits of vanilla beans and extracts in Africa are diverse and impressive. Reimagining this beloved flavor in various culinary delights, harnessing its health benefits, utilizing it in beauty and relaxation therapies, and providing a livelihood for vanilla farmers, vanilla is truly a gift to Africa. Embracing this incredible ingredient not only enhances African traditions and cuisine but also supports sustainable development and economic growth throughout the continent.

- The examples and recipes of cocktails using vanilla in Africa

Vanilla is a versatile and aromatic ingredient that adds depth and complexity to cocktails. Often associated with sweet desserts, this exotic spice can also enhance the flavors of African-inspired beverages. In this article, we will explore a few examples and provide recipes of cocktails that incorporate vanilla, showcasing the rich and diverse flavors of the African continent.

1. Rooibos and Vanilla Iced Tea Cocktail:
Inspired by the bold flavors of South Africa, this refreshing cocktail combines the earthy notes of rooibos with the sweet warmth of vanilla. Here's how to make it:

Ingredients:
- 1 cup brewed rooibos tea, chilled
- 2 oz vodka
- 1 oz vanilla-infused simple syrup (combine equal parts vanilla extract, sugar, and water, simmer until sugar dissolves, then let cool)
- Fresh mint leaves (for garnish)
- Ice cubes

Instructions:
1. Fill a glass with ice cubes.
2. In a cocktail shaker, combine the chilled rooibos tea, vodka, and vanilla-infused simple syrup.
3. Shake vigorously for a few seconds, then strain the mixture into the prepared glass.
4. Garnish with fresh mint leaves and enjoy the invigorating flavors of South Africa in every sip.

2. Moroccan Spice Martini:
Transport yourself to the vibrant streets of Marrakech with this sumptuous martini infused with the exotic spices of the region, including vanilla. This

craft cocktail is perfect for those seeking a unique flavor experience. Here's how to create it:

Ingredients:
- 2 oz spiced rum
- 1 oz orange liqueur
- 1/2 oz lemon juice
- 1/4 oz vanilla syrup
- Pinch of ground cinnamon
- Ice cubes
- Orange twist (for garnish)

Instructions:
1. Fill a cocktail shaker with ice cubes.
2. Add the spiced rum, orange liqueur, lemon juice, vanilla syrup, and a pinch of ground cinnamon to the shaker.
3. Shake vigorously until well-chilled and strain the mixture into a martini glass.
4. Garnish with an orange twist for an elegant touch and savor the tantalizing blend of Moroccan spices enriched by the smoothness of vanilla.

3. Amarula Vanilla Mule:
Amarula, a cream liqueur made from the fruit of the African marula tree, takes center stage in this delightful twist on the classic Moscow Mule. The addition of vanilla elevates this cocktail to new heights of lusciousness. Here's how to make it:

Ingredients:
- 2 oz Amarula liqueur
- 1/2 oz lime juice
- 4 oz ginger beer
- Ice cubes
- Lime wedge (for garnish)
- Vanilla bean for stirring

Instructions:
1. Fill a copper mug or glass with ice cubes.

2. Pour the Amarula liqueur and lime juice over the ice.
3. Top it off with ginger beer and gently stir with a vanilla bean.
4. Garnish with a lime wedge and enjoy the creamy indulgence of the African savannah with every sip.

Adding a touch of vanilla to your African-inspired cocktails can truly transform their flavors, creating a memorable sensory experience. Experiment with the provided recipes, or let them inspire you to create your own unique concoctions that celebrate the cultural richness of Africa. Cheers to crafting and savoring delicious vanilla-infused cocktails on your global drinking adventures!

Chapter 15: Saffron - The Origin and Distribution of Saffron in Africa

Saffron, a vibrant and captivating spice, renowned for its distinct flavor, color, and aroma, has a rich history dating back millennia. Its origins can be traced to ancient Iran and Greece, where it was highly valued for its medicinal and culinary properties. However, many are unaware of the fascinating journey and distribution of saffron in Africa. This chapter aims to shed light on the origins, cultivation, and distribution of saffron in various regions of Africa, exploring its impact on local culture, economics, and tradition.

Saffron's Arrival in Africa
The arrival of saffron in Africa can be attributed to various factors, including trade routes, conquests, and migrations. It is believed that during the Roman period, saffron made its way to North Africa through trade networks connecting the Mediterranean coasts. These networks facilitated the exchange of goods, ideas, and even botanical specimens, enabling the dissemination of saffron across the African continent.

Western Africa: Morocco and Algeria
Morocco and Algeria, situated in North Africa, have a long history of saffron cultivation. Here, saffron production dates back to the 8th century, with the Toubkal region in Morocco becoming one of the largest saffron producers in Africa. The favorable climate, with its cold winters and arid summers, coupled with the region's rich soil, makes it an ideal location for growing this prized spice. Today, saffron production continues to thrive in these regions, contributing significantly to the local agricultural economy.

Eastern Africa: Ethiopia
The highlands of Ethiopia offer another intriguing chapter in the African saffron story. Traditionally known as "Ethiopian Gold," saffron cultivars

native to the region boast unique characteristics, distinct from their Mediterranean counterparts. With its high altitudes and temperate climate, Ethiopia has emerged as a promising saffron-growing region. The region's saffron industry is largely concentrated in the Amhara and Tigray regions, and its impact on the local economy is steadily growing.

Southern Africa: South Africa and Zimbabwe
In recent years, saffron production has started gaining momentum in Southern Africa. South Africa and Zimbabwe have seen a surge in saffron cultivation, driven by factors such as favorable climatic conditions, government support, and an increasing demand for organic and niche products. The Cederberg Mountains in South Africa and the highlands of Zimbabwe have become fertile grounds for saffron cultivation, providing new economic opportunities and cultural exchanges in these regions.

Cultural Significance of Saffron in Africa
Saffron has not only made its mark in African cuisine but is deeply rooted in the cultural fabric of various African communities. Its inclusion in traditional dishes, rituals, and herbal remedies reflects its esteemed status across different cultures. Additionally, the vibrant red color of saffron has inspired traditional crafts, woven fabrics, and even local art forms, showcasing the significant role it plays in African aesthetics and creativity.

Challenges and Future Prospects
While the distribution of saffron in Africa has shown considerable growth and potential, it also faces numerous challenges. Climate change, land availability, and lack of technological advancements pose significant obstacles in sustaining and expanding saffron production. Nevertheless, ongoing research, collaborations, and increased awareness about the economic and cultural value of saffron in Africa hold great promise. With proper support and investment, African countries have the potential to become pivotal players in the global saffron industry.

The distribution of saffron in Africa unveils a fascinating tale woven into the fabric of the continent's history, culture, and economic development. From its ancient arrival through trade routes to its present-day cultivation in regions like Morocco, Ethiopia, South Africa, and Zimbabwe, saffron continues to captivate and inspire. As Africa showcases its saffron potential, it reminds the world of the spice's profound impact, transcendence of borders, and ability to enhance not only flavors but also the lives of those involved in its production.

- The uses and benefits of saffron threads and powder in Africa

The Uses and Benefits of Saffron Threads and Powder in Africa

Saffron, derived from the flower of Crocus sativus, is a highly esteemed spice known for its vibrant color, unique flavor, and medicinal properties. While it is primarily associated with regions like Iran, Spain, and India, saffron's uses and benefits are not limited to these areas. This article aims to explore the various applications and advantages of saffron threads and powder specifically in Africa, shedding light on the presence and importance of this valuable spice on the continent.

1. Culinary Uses:
(a) Flavor Enhancement: Saffron adds a distinct flavor and aroma to a wide range of African cuisines. It is particularly popular in North African dishes such as Moroccan tagines, Tunisian couscous, and Egyptian tea.
(b) Coloring Agent: With its breathtaking crimson hue, saffron naturally dyes culinary creations including rice, biryanis, stews, bread, desserts, and spicy sauces, uplifting the visual appeal of dishes and elevating the overall dining experience.

2. Medicinal and Therapeutic Applications:
(a) Traditional Medicine: For ages, saffron has been recognized as a potent traditional remedy for various ailments. It is used in Africa to alleviate symptoms of digestive disorders, improve circulation, and mitigate

menstrual pain.
(b) Antioxidant and Anti-inflammatory Properties: Saffron is rich in carotenoids, bioactive compounds that act as antioxidants, protecting cells from damage caused by harmful free radicals. Additionally, it has inherent anti-inflammatory characteristics, potentially aiding in the treatment of conditions like arthritis and certain cardiovascular diseases.

3. Cosmetics and Beauty:
(a) Skin Remedies: The smoothening and lightening properties of saffron make it an ideal ingredient in various skincare products, serving as an effective treatment against acne, blemishes, dark circles, and sun damage.
(b) Relaxation and Wellness: Saffron has calming and mood-enhancing properties. It is used in Africa for skincare, aromatherapy, and relaxation due to its pleasant scent, allowing individuals to unwind and improve both mental and physical well-being.

4. Cultural Significance:
(a) Traditional Celebrations: Saffron represents opulence and auspiciousness in several African cultures. It is used to prepare special dishes and beverages during weddings, festivals, and holidays, making it an integral part of the country's rich cultural heritage.
(b) Social Bonding: The process of harvesting saffron itself is labor-intensive and requires significant manpower. This has fostered a sense of community and bonding, as families and groups come together during the harvest season, reinforcing social relationships and preserving cultural traditions.

Saffron, with its diverse uses, medicinal properties, and cultural significance, plays a significant role in Africa's gastronomy, traditional practices, and overall well-being. From enhancing the flavors of local dishes to adding vibrancy to celebrations, this precious spice continues to be an essential part of African cuisine, culture, and everyday life.

- The examples and recipes of cocktails using saffron in Africa

Saffron, the golden spice derived from the flower of Crocus sativus, has been widely used in various cuisines for centuries. While it is commonly associated with Mediterranean and Middle Eastern cuisines, saffron also holds significance in African culinary traditions. With its aromatic and unique flavor, saffron is often used to enhance the taste and appearance of dishes, and even find its way into cocktails. In this article, we will explore some fascinating examples and recipes of cocktails using saffron in Africa.

1. Touareg Saffron Tea Mule:
Originating from North Africa, this cocktail takes inspiration from the traditional Touareg tea. To make this refreshing saffron-infused drink, you will need:

Ingredients:
- 4 saffron threads
- 2 ounces of vodka
- 1 ounce of ginger beer
- 1/2 ounce of fresh lime juice
- 1/2 ounce of simple syrup
- Ice cubes
- Lime slices, for garnish

Instructions:
1. Crush the saffron threads in a small glass and add a tablespoon of warm water. Let it steep for 10 minutes, allowing the vibrant color and aroma to infuse.
2. In a cocktail shaker, combine the saffron infusion, vodka, lime juice, and simple syrup. Shake well to mix.
3. Fill a serving glass with ice cubes and strain the cocktail mixture over it.
4. Top it off with ginger beer and garnish with lime slices. Serve and enjoy!

2. Saharan Sunset Mojito:
Inspired by the breathtaking sunsets stretching over the Sahara Desert, this saffron-infused mojito boasts flavors that transport you to Africa. To create this vibrant cocktail, here's what you'll need:

Ingredients:
- 8-10 fresh mint leaves
- 4 saffron threads
- 2 ounces of aged rum
- 1 ounce of fresh lime juice
- 1 ounce of simple syrup
- Club soda
- Lime wedges and mint sprigs, for garnish

Instructions:
1. Muddle fresh mint leaves and saffron threads in a cocktail shaker to release their aromas and flavors.
2. Add aged rum, lime juice, and simple syrup to the shaker. Shake well to combine the ingredients.
3. Fill a highball glass with ice cubes and strain the cocktail mixture into it.
4. Top it with a splash of club soda and garnish with lime wedges and mint sprigs. Sip and savor the Saharan flavors in this refreshing mojito.

3. Saffron Soirée Martini:
This elegant cocktail showcases the richness of saffron and perfectly brings a touch of luxury to any evening. Here's what you will need to create this exquisite drink:

Ingredients:
- 6 saffron threads
- 2 ounces of gin
- 1/2 ounce of dry vermouth
- Ice cubes
- Lemon twist, for garnish

Instructions:
1. Place the saffron threads in a martini glass and let them steep in 1/2 ounce

of warm water for 10 minutes to develop their flavors and color.
2. In a mixing glass, combine the saffron infusion, gin, and dry vermouth. Stir well.
3. Fill a separate martini glass with ice cubes to chill it for a minute or two, then discard the ice.
4. Strain the cocktail mixture into the chilled martini glass and garnish with a twist of lemon. Sip and savor the sophistication of this saffron soirée martini.

The utilization of saffron in African cocktails allows us to enjoy the distinct flavors and vibrant colors this spice brings, adding an exotic touch to our mixology adventures. So toast to the tales of Africa while exploring the fascinating world of saffron-infused cocktails and elevate your taste experience with these enticing recipes.

Chapter 16: Palm Wine - The Origin and Distribution of Palm Wine in Africa

Palm wine, known by various names such as toddy, palm sap, and wine of the palms, is a traditional alcoholic beverage that has been consumed for centuries in Africa. This chapter explores the origins and distribution of palm wine in Africa, shedding light on the cultural, economic, and historical significance of this beverage.

1. Historical Origins:
Palm wine has a rich history in Africa, with evidence of its consumption dating back several millennia. It is believed to have originated in West Africa and gradually spread to other regions of the continent. The early African civilizations, such as the Kingdom of Ghana and Mali, treasured palm wine and used it as a symbol of wealth and prestige.

2. Palms Species:
Palm wine is typically extracted from a variety of palm trees that are native to Africa. Some of the most commonly used palm species include the oil palm (Elaeis guineensis), the date palm (Phoenix dactylifera), and the raffia palm (Raphia spp.). Each palm species contributes unique flavors and characteristics to the resulting palm wine.

3. Extraction Process:
The process of obtaining palm wine involves tapping the tree and collecting the sap, which naturally flows from the incisions made on the trunk. This sap is then fermented by natural yeasts present in the environment, resulting in the transformation of the sweet sap into an alcoholic beverage. The extraction process requires skill and knowledge, as the collection must be carefully managed to avoid damaging the tree.

4. Cultural and Social Significance:
Palm wine holds immense cultural and social significance in African

societies. It is often consumed during celebrations, ceremonies, and social gatherings, forming an integral part of various rituals. Palm wine is believed to foster community bonding, symbolize hospitality, and connect individuals with their ancestral roots.

5. Economic Importance:
Apart from its social and cultural value, palm wine has a substantial economic impact in many African countries. Small-scale palm wine production and trade can provide a steady income for rural communities. In some areas, it has even evolved into a commercial venture, with palm wine becoming an export commodity.

6. Distribution and Consumption Patterns:
Palm wine is widely consumed across the African continent, spanning numerous countries and cultures. It is particularly prevalent in West and Central Africa, where it is regarded as a regional specialty. Within these regions, variations in palm wine production techniques, flavors, and cultural practices exist, reflecting the local diversity and heritage.

7. Modern Challenges:
Despite its historical and cultural significance, palm wine faces challenges in the modern era. Changing lifestyles, urbanization, and the expansion of beverage industries have led to a decline in traditional palm wine production. Additionally, unsustainable harvesting practices and deforestation pose threats to palm tree populations, highlighting the need for sustainable management and conservation efforts.

Palm wine, being deeply ingrained in the heritage of Africa, deserves recognition for its historical, cultural, and economic contributions. Understanding the origin and distribution of palm wine not only offers insights into African traditions, but it also highlights the importance of safeguarding this ancient practice for future generations. As we delve further into the study of palm wine, it becomes evident that this fermented beverage holds a special place in the diverse tapestry of African cultures.

- The production and consumption of palm wine in Africa

Palm wine, also known as "palm sap" or "toddy," has been a staple beverage in Africa for centuries. This mildly intoxicating drink is extracted from the sap of various species of palm trees and is consumed fresh or fermented. The production and consumption of palm wine play a significant cultural and economic role in many African communities.

The process of palm wine production begins with the careful selection of the palm tree. Trees that are at least 10 years old and have a circumference of about 2 to 3 feet are ideal for tapping. Some of the commonly used palm tree species include the African oil palm, the date palm, and the Raffia palm. These trees are widely cultivated across the continent, providing a sustainable source of sap.

To harvest palm sap, traditional tappers climb the palm trees and skillfully tie bamboo containers, called calabash or gourd shells, tightly around the budding flower stalk or the inflorescence. The sap gradually accumulates inside these containers over a period of approximately 24 to 48 hours. Tappers typically revisit the same tree every day to collect the fresh sap before it spoils.

The collected palm sap is sweet and naturally non-alcoholic. However, it begins fermenting rapidly due to local yeasts and wild microbes present in the surroundings. Fermentation can occur in the calabash containers or may be transferred to larger containers like barrels or earthen pots. Fermentation gives palm wine its characteristic alcoholic content and flavor.

Fermentation can take anywhere from a few hours to several days, depending on environmental factors such as temperature and microbial activity. During this process, the sugar in the sap is transformed into alcohol. The longer the fermentation period, the stronger the palm wine becomes. It typically ranges from a mildly carbonated, sweet beverage with an alcohol content of around 2%-4% to a stronger, more acidic drink with an alcohol content of up to 6%-8%.

Palm wine consumption is deeply ingrained in African culture. In many communities, it serves as a symbolic drink during various ceremonies, rituals, and celebrations. It is often shared among family, friends, and neighbors, promoting communal bonds and social cohesion. Palm wine is culturally significant for its association with fertility, abundance, and communal well-being.

Beyond cultural significance, palm wine production also plays a role in the local economy. The tapping and processing of palm wine provide income for thousands of people across rural Africa. Small-scale farmers, usually from the poorest regions, engage in the sale of palm wine as an alternative livelihood source. It has become a small industry of its own, supporting rural families and contributing to local economies.

While palm wine continues to be a cherished and widely consumed beverage in Africa, there are concerns about sustainability and impacts on palm tree populations. Indiscriminate tapping and overharvesting pose a threat to the livelihood of palm trees and forest ecosystems. Efforts are underway to encourage responsible and sustainable palm wine production to preserve both the cultural significance and ecological health associated with this ancient tradition.

In conclusion, the production and consumption of palm wine in Africa have a rich history and cultural significance. This traditional beverage not only holds a prominent place in various African ceremonies and rituals but also contributes to local economies. It is a testament to the profound connection between nature, culture, and sustainable livelihoods in African communities, making palm wine an irreplaceable part of the continent's heritage.

- The examples and recipes of cocktails using palm wine in Africa

In Africa, palm wine is not only a beloved beverage but also a popular ingredient in many traditional cocktails. Derived from various palm tree species, such as the African oil palm, date palm, and the sapodilla tree, palm wine holds a special place in the hearts and glasses of the African people. Let's explore some fascinating examples and delightful recipes showcasing the versatility and unique flavors of cocktails made with palm wine.

1. Palm Wine Punch: This refreshing punch combines the tropical flavors of palm wine with a zesty citrus twist. To prepare this cocktail, start by mixing one cup of palm wine with the juice of one lemon, lime, and orange. Add a splash of pineapple juice and a teaspoon of honey for a touch of sweetness. Stir in some ice cubes and garnish with slices of fresh citrus fruit and a sprig of mint. The Palm Wine Punch is ideal for warm summer evenings.

2. Coco-Wine Daiquiri: Put an African spin on the classic daiquiri by substituting rum with rich palm wine. Begin by blending two cups of ice, half a cup of palm wine, two tablespoons of coconut cream, one tablespoon of lime juice, and a teaspoon of simple syrup (optional) until smooth. Rim a chilled glass with shredded coconut, pour the daiquiri mixture, and garnish with a lime wedge or a pineapple slice. Sip this tropical delight and transport yourself to an exotic paradise.

3. Masala Palm Wine Mojito: Enter the world of aromatic spices and magical flavors with this fusion cocktail. In a glass, muddle a few fresh mint leaves along with the juice of half a lime and a teaspoon of brown sugar. Add a quarter teaspoon each of ground cinnamon and cardamom powder, and a pinch of grated nutmeg. Pour in ⅔ cup of palm wine and top up the glass with soda water. Stir gently, garnish with a mint sprig, and enjoy the captivating taste of this Masala Palm Wine Mojito.

4. Tigernut Palm Wine Shake: Explore the rich African culinary heritage with

this creamy and satisfying shake. Combine one cup of tiger nut milk (or substitute with almond or cashew milk), half a cup of palm wine, a ripe banana, a tablespoon of honey, and a handful of ice cubes in a blender. Blend until smooth and frothy. Serve in a tall glass garnished with shaved chocolate or crushed tigernuts. This nutritious shake is perfect for breakfast or as a nutritious treat any time of the day.

5. Nigerian Palm Wine Cocktail: This cocktail highlights the traditional Nigerian flavors of palm wine with a delicious twist. In a shaker, combine two ounces of palm wine, one ounce of ginger liqueur, half an ounce of freshly squeezed lime or lemon juice, and a dash of Angostura bitters. Shake vigorously with ice and strain into a chilled glass. Garnish with a slice of ginger or lime zest for an added touch of elegance. Savor the unique taste of this cocktail that embodies the spirit of Nigerian traditions.

These examples and recipes are just a glimpse into the treasure trove of cocktail creations incorporating the unique taste of palm wine in Africa. Whether you're enjoying the tropics, the spices, or the sweet aromas, these cocktails offer a delightful way to immerse yourself in the diverse African drinking culture and experience the flavors of this ancient palm tree elixir. So raise a glass and embark on a flavorful adventure with palm wine cocktails!

Chapter 17: Sorghum Beer - The Origin and Distribution of Sorghum Beer in Africa

Sorghum beer, one of Africa's most renowned traditional alcoholic beverages, holds a significant historical and cultural importance across the continent. This chapter aims to explore the fascinating origins and distribution of sorghum beer in Africa, unraveling its place as a communal drink that has stood the test of time.

1. Historical Context:
1.1 Ancient roots of sorghum beer:
The practice of brewing sorghum beer traces back thousands of years to ancient African civilizations. Archaeological evidence suggests that sorghum, the primary ingredient in this beer, was domesticated in Africa around 3000 BCE, highlighting its indigenous origins.

1.2 Ritual and ceremonial use:
Throughout history, sorghum beer has played a crucial role in African rituals and ceremonies. It was often used in ceremonies related to birth, marriage, initiation, and ancestral worship. These events were not only social occasions but were considered sacred and vital in maintaining the communal fabric of African society.

2. Brewing Traditions:
2.1 Traditional brewing processes:
The production of sorghum beer involves intricate brewing techniques passed down through generations. The sorghum grains are milled, germinated, and then malted. After malting, they are boiled, cooled, and mixed with water to facilitate fermentation. Natural strains of yeast, present in the environment or added deliberately, aid in the fermenting process. The end result is a frothy, slightly sour, and richly flavored beer.

2.2 Regional variations:

Different regions in Africa have developed their unique variations of sorghum beer, each with its distinct flavors and brewing methods. Some widely recognized types include Pito in Nigeria and Ghana, Umqombothi in South Africa, and Tella in Ethiopia. These regional variations add depth to the cultural diversity surrounding sorghum beer.

3. Socio-cultural Significance:
3.1 Communal bonding:
Sorghum beer acts as a symbol of unity, bringing people together in celebrations, gatherings, and social interactions. It fosters communal bonding, reinforcing traditional values, and perpetuating cultural identity. In many African communities, the brewing process itself represents a communal effort, with women often taking on the responsibility.

3.2 Economic importance:
Sorghum beer also holds economic importance, especially in rural areas, where it serves as an income source for many households. The brewing and selling of sorghum beer create a means of survival, employment, and entrepreneurship for women and youth, contributing to local economies.

4. Challenges and Opportunities:
4.1 Industrialization and commercialization:
The rise of modern brewing techniques, commercial breweries, and the global alcohol industry pose challenges to traditional sorghum beer. However, this shift also presents opportunities for preserving traditional methods while adapting to new market demands.

4.2 Gender dynamics:
Within the context of sorghum beer brewing, there exist gender dynamics that can both empower and constrain women. Exploring these dynamics helps create an understanding of how advancements in gender equality can maintain cultural heritage while promoting inclusivity.

Sorghum beer, deeply rooted in African culture, is more than just a drink; it embodies tradition, ritual, and communal harmony. Its origin and distribution connect African societies and celebrations, weaving a tapestry of flavors and techniques across the continent. The challenges faced by sorghum beer throughout history present opportunities for preservation and adaptation, ensuring it continues to be a thriving aspect of African heritage.

- The production and consumption of sorghum beer in Africa

Sorghum beer is a traditional alcoholic beverage that has been produced and consumed in Africa for centuries. The beverage is made from sorghum, a type of grain that is widely cultivated and used as a staple food crop in many parts of the continent.

The production process of sorghum beer varies among different African regions, but the basic steps remain the same. Firstly, the sorghum grains are soaked in water for a certain period of time to allow them to germinate. This germination process triggers the production of natural enzymes in the grains that help to break down starches into fermentable sugars.

After germination, the grains are spread out to dry before being milled into a coarse flour. This flour, known as malted sorghum, is then mixed with hot water and left to steep for several hours. During this time, the starches in the flour are converted into sugars by the enzymes produced during germination.

Once the enzymatic conversion is complete, the mixture is strained to separate the liquid portion from the leftover grains. The liquid, known as the wort, is transferred into a fermentation vessel and allowed to cool. At this point, a starter culture of wild yeast is introduced to kick-start the fermentation process.

Fermentation generally takes place in large clay pots or plastic containers. The wild yeast consumes the sugars in the wort and converts them into alcohol and carbon dioxide. The fermentation process can take anywhere from a few days to a couple of weeks, depending on various factors such as temperature and yeast activity.

After fermentation, the sorghum beer is traditionally served either freshly brewed or after being stored for a short period of time to allow for further maturation. The final product is low in alcohol content, typically ranging from 1% to 4%, and has a slightly sour taste with some notes of sweetness and a mellow maltiness.

Sorghum beer holds a significant cultural and social significance in many African communities. It is often consumed during social gatherings, traditional ceremonies, and rites of passage. It serves as a symbol of hospitality and community bonding, bringing people together to share stories, laughter, and experiences.

In addition to its cultural value, sorghum beer also has economic importance in Africa. Local breweries and vendors play a vital role in producing and distributing the beverage, providing livelihoods to many individuals and contributing to the local economy. Moreover, the production of sorghum as a raw material for the beer industry creates income opportunities for farmers, thereby promoting a sustainable agricultural sector.

However, the consumption and production of sorghum beer is not without challenges. In some regions, the traditional methods of production lack adequate hygiene standards, resulting in potential health risks. Efforts are being made to improve these practices, incorporating modern techniques that ensure safety and quality throughout the production process.

Furthermore, with the rise of industrialized brewing, commercial beers have gained popularity over traditional sorghum beer in urban areas, leading to a decline in demand. Efforts are underway to promote and market sorghum beer as a unique and authentic African beverage, increasing its visibility and consumption both domestically and internationally.

Overall, the production and consumption of sorghum beer in Africa is a fascinating aspect of the continent's rich cultural heritage. It showcases the ingenuity of African communities in utilizing local resources to create unique and flavorful beverages, while also contributing to the social and economic fabric of the region.

- The examples and recipes of cocktails using sorghum beer in Africa

In Africa, sorghum beer has a long history and significance in many cultures. This traditional beer, also known as ingudu, bilibili, pombe, or dolo, has been brewed for centuries using sorghum, a primary cereal crop in the continent. Known for its distinct flavors and unique brewing methods, sorghum beer is a prominent feature in African social gatherings and festivities.

One of the most common variations of sorghum beer is Umqombothi, a traditional drink from South Africa. It is made by fermenting sorghum malt with various other ingredients like maize, yeast, and water. Umqombothi is a thick, white and sour beer that offers a refreshing taste.

Another flavorful concoction is Burukutu, a Nigerian beer made from fermented sorghum or millet. Burukutu is celebrated for its balanced bittersweet taste and is often flavored with fruits or roots like pineapple or ginger.

Moving further east, in Ethiopia, we have the iconic Tella. This beer is produced using fermented sorghum grains and sometimes oats or barley. Tella is a key component in Ethiopian culture and plays a significant role during festivals, weddings, and even religious events.

One example from Western Africa is Dolo, which is popular in countries like Mali, Ivory Coast, and Burkina Faso. This traditional sorghum beer is known for its earthy and sour taste. Dolo is typically brewed by women in villages and is consumed both for enjoyment and as a source of income.

Now that we have explored a few examples of sorghum beer varieties found across Africa, let's dive into recipes for some delightful cocktails that incorporate this unique brew:

1. Sorghum Shandy:
- 1 bottle of sorghum beer
- 1/2 cup of lemonade or ginger ale
- Slices of lemon or lime for garnish

In a glass, mix the sorghum beer and lemonade or ginger ale. Stir gently to combine. Add ice cubes and garnish with lemon or lime slices.

2. Sorghum Sunrise:
- 1/2 cup of sorghum beer
- 1/4 cup of orange juice
- 1 tablespoon of grenadine syrup
- Orange slice for garnish

In a glass, combine the sorghum beer, orange juice, and grenadine syrup. Stir until well-mixed. Add ice cubes and garnish with an orange slice.

3. African Mule:
- 1/2 cup of sorghum beer
- 1 1/2 ounces of vodka
- 1/4 cup of ginger beer
- Fresh mint leaves for garnish

In a copper mug filled with ice, combine the sorghum beer, vodka, and ginger beer. Stir gently and garnish with fresh mint leaves.

4. Dolo Delight:
- 1 cup of cold dolo (sorghum beer)
- 1/4 cup of pineapple juice
- 1/4 cup of coconut milk
- Pineapple slice for garnish

In a shaker, combine the cold dolo, pineapple juice, and coconut milk. Shake well and strain into a glass filled with ice cubes. Garnish with a pineapple slice.

These are just a few examples of cocktails that incorporate the unique flavors of sorghum beer found in Africa. The versatility of this traditional brew allows for endless possibilities, making it an exciting ingredient to explore in mixology.

Chapter 18: Honey Wine- The Origin and Distribution of Honey Wine in Africa

Honey wine, also known as mead, is a traditional alcoholic drink made by fermenting honey with water. It has a fascinating history that dates back several thousand years. In this chapter, we will explore the origin and distribution of honey wine in Africa, shedding light on its cultural significance and how it has evolved over time.

The Origin of Honey Wine in Africa:
Africa is often regarded as the birthplace of honey wine, with evidence suggesting that it has been consumed on the continent for at least 20,000 years. The iconic rock paintings found in the Drakensberg Mountains of South Africa depict scenes of honey gathering, indicating that early African civilizations were familiar with the production and consumption of honey-based beverages.

The indigenous African people, particularly those living in regions such as Ethiopia, Sudan, and the Democratic Republic of Congo, were among the first to ferment honey into a potent alcoholic beverage. The practice of making honey wine was intricately connected to their cultural and religious rituals, with the drink often being used in ceremonial events, weddings, and festive celebrations.

Distribution of Honey Wine across Africa:
As African civilizations expanded and connected with one another through trade and cultural exchanges, the distribution of honey wine spread throughout the continent. Different regions developed their unique ways of making honey wine, resulting in a wide variety of styles and flavors.

In East Africa, particularly in Ethiopia, honey wine called "Tej" is a prominent cultural beverage. It is made by fermenting honey with the addition of water and a mixture of herbs and spices, including gesho, a plant native to the region. Tej is still commonly consumed in traditional Ethiopian households and is even recognized as the national drink of the country.

In West Africa, the indigenous people have their version of honey wine known as "Ogol." This drink is made by fermenting honey with water, followed by the addition of various local fruits, roots, and grains to enhance the flavor. The recipe for Ogol varies from region to region, with each area adding its unique twist to the beverage.

In Southern Africa, the San people, also known as Bushmen, have a long-standing tradition of making honey wine. They construct bee traps to gather honey and ferment it in ostrich eggshells buried in the sand. This method of preparation adds a distinctly earthy taste to their honey wine, making it one of a kind.

The Cultural Significance of Honey Wine in Africa:
Honey wine holds immense cultural significance in African societies. It is often used as an offering to ancestors and spirits, thus serving as a vital link between the living and the spiritual world. This drink is also an integral part of tribal rituals and ceremonies, symbolizing fertility, abundance, and prosperity.

Furthermore, honey wine plays a role in social gatherings and storytelling events. It acts as a bonding agent, bringing people together and fostering a sense of unity and communal identity. Songs and dances are performed during the consumption of honey wine, creating an atmosphere of joy and celebration.

Modern Era and Commercial Production:
With the advent of modern brewing techniques and globalization, honey wine production has undergone significant changes. While traditional methods are still practiced in some rural areas, commercial breweries have emerged in various African countries, producing honey wine for both domestic and international markets.

These commercial breweries often incorporate modern equipment and innovations, allowing for mass production of honey wine. However, the authentic flavors and rituals associated with homemade honey wine remain deeply embedded within African culture and continue to be cherished by traditional enthusiasts and connoisseurs.

Africa has a rich history and cultural heritage when it comes to honey wine production. The practice of fermenting honey into a delightful beverage traces back thousands of years and has been an essential part of various cultural and religious ceremonies. Today, honey wine is not merely a drink but a symbol of African tradition, spirituality, and communal unity. Its ever-evolving techniques and diverse flavors contribute to its enduring popularity both within the continent and beyond.

- The production and consumption of honey wine in Africa

In Africa, the production and consumption of honey wine, also known as mead, holds a long and rich history. Dating back thousands of years, honey wine has played a significant role in traditional African cultures and continues to be enjoyed by many individuals today. Let's delve into the fascinating world of honey wine in Africa, exploring its production methods, cultural significance, and consumption patterns.

The production of honey wine in Africa is a labor-intensive process that requires careful craftsmanship and ancient knowledge passed down through generations. Honey, the main ingredient, is meticulously collected from beehives located in specific regions known for their diverse floral landscapes. These areas often have a wide variety of flowering plants, such as acacia, baobab, and wildflowers, which contribute to the distinct flavor profiles of African mead.

Traditionally, African beekeepers utilized woven baskets or clay pots as beehives, with some tribes even cultivating their own unique species of honeybee. This symbiotic relationship between humans and bees has fostered a deep understanding of sustainable honey harvesting practices, ensuring the preservation of both the bees and their natural environment.

Once the honey is harvested, it undergoes a fermentation process. The honey is typically diluted with water to create a honey-water mixture known as must, which is then left to naturally ferment. This process can take anywhere from a few weeks to several months, during which wild yeasts present in the environment transform the sugars in the honey into alcohol. Some African communities add additional ingredients to enhance the fermentation process, such as bark, herbs, or spices, further enhancing the unique character of the honey wine.

The final product of this meticulous production process is a golden-hued wine with varying levels of sweetness and complexity. It often possesses distinct floral and fruity flavors, with some regional variations adding earthy or herbal undertones. Unlike grape-based wines, honey wine tends to have a higher alcohol content, ranging from 10-20% alcohol by volume (ABV). However, specific alcohol levels vary depending on the fermentation process and the preferences of the local community.

Honey wine production in Africa extends beyond its gastronomic aspects. Throughout African history, mead has been deeply intertwined with cultural traditions, religious practices, and social gatherings. In many African societies, honey wine holds symbolic value and is used in ceremonies and rituals to celebrate major life events like weddings, births, or harvest festivals. It is often believed to have magical or healing properties, making it an essential part of traditional medicine and spiritual practices. Even today, honey wine continues to be shared among friends and family during important social gatherings and feasts, fostering a sense of community and celebration.

In terms of consumption patterns, the popularity of honey wine in Africa varies across different regions and communities. In some arid areas where agricultural production is challenging, honey wine has long served as a staple beverage. The Maasai tribe in Kenya, for instance, highly values honey wine and incorporates it into their daily diet. Additionally, certain African countries, such as Ethiopia, South Africa, and Nigeria, have their own rich mead-drinking cultures, with dedicated mead halls and markets catering to enthusiasts.

Recently, there has been a resurgence of interest in honey wine within the global craft beverage industry market. African honey wines are garnering attention for their distinct flavors, quality, and unique storytelling capabilities. This newfound appreciation has led to the establishment of boutique wineries and meaderies, with African honey wines gaining recognition on the international stage.

The production and consumption of honey wine in Africa embody the continent's cultural heritage, rich biodiversity, and centuries-old practices of beekeeping. It continues to serve as a potent symbol of unity, spirituality, and shared joy among African communities. As interest in honey wine continues to grow both locally and globally, it is hoped that the traditions and knowledge surrounding its production are safeguarded and celebrated for generations to come.

- The examples and recipes of cocktails using honey wine in Africa

Honey Wine Delights: A Celebration of African Cocktails

African cultures have embraced the art of brewing for centuries, creating various types of traditional alcoholic beverages. Among these revered brews is honey wine, a tantalizing elixir made from honey, water, and sometimes combined with different fruits, herbs, and spices. While honey wine is often enjoyed on its own, it also shines as a versatile ingredient in many exotic cocktails. Join us on a journey through Africa's cocktails as we uncover unique recipes and examples of incorporating honey wine to awaken your taste buds.

1. Mkie, the Tanzanian Breeze:
This refreshing cocktail from Tanzania brings together the aromatic notes of honey wine with tropical flavors. To create the Mkie, mix 1.5 oz of honey wine with 2 oz of fresh pineapple juice. Add a squeeze of lime juice, a splash of grenadine, and a handful of ice cubes. Shake well and strain into a chilled martini glass. Garnish with a pineapple wedge, and embark on a sip that transports you to the lush landscapes of East Africa.

2. Cape Safari, an African Sunset:
South Africa's vibrant cocktail scene invites you to experience the marvelous Cape Safari. Crafted by combining 2 oz of honey wine, 1 oz of citrus vodka, 1.5 oz of cranberry juice, and a dash of orange bitters, this colorful cocktail embodies the warmth of a dust-kissed sunset over the Cape of Good Hope. Shake all ingredients with ice, strain into a tumbler glass, and garnish with an orange twist for an invigorating taste of Southern African glamour.

3. Nile Mule, an Egyptian Twist:
Drawing inspiration from the rich heritage of Egypt, the Nile Mule demonstrates the art of balancing flavors. Combine 2 oz of honey wine, half an ounce of vodka, half a squeezed lime, and a splash of ginger beer in a copper mug or highball glass filled with ice. Stir gently and garnish with a lime wheel and a fresh sprig of mint for a zesty cocktail that evokes spiritual whispers along the banks of the Nile.

4. Kigali Cosmo, Rwanda Rendezvous:
Capturing the heart and urban vibe of Rwanda, the Kigali Cosmo will elevate any moment. Mix 1.5 oz of honey wine, 1 oz of triple sec, a squeeze of fresh lime juice, and 2 oz of unsweetened cranberry juice in a shaker with ice. Shake vigorously and strain into a chilled martini glass. Garnish with a lime twist, and toast to the spirit of reconciliation and progress embodied by the city of Kigali.

5. Botswana Blossom, the Jewel of the Kalahari:
Inspired by the mesmerizing colors of Botswana's Kalahari Desert, this cocktail transforms honey wine into a sensual masterpiece. Mix 2 oz of honey wine, 1.5 oz of bourbon, 0.5 oz of fresh lemon juice, and a teaspoon of

grenadine syrup in a cocktail shaker with ice. Shake, strain into a rocks glass filled with ice, and garnish with a twisted lemon peel. Celebrate the inner strength of collaboration, shimmering in the heart of the African wilderness.

Awaken your senses with the richness of African cocktails using honey wine. These examples transport you across the continent, offering a taste of Tanzania's tropics, South African sunsets, Egyptian ancient wonders, Rwandan courage, and Botswana's arid beauty. Venture into the world of honey wine mixology to discover unique dimensions of flavor and celebrate the diversity and creativity ingrained in the African cocktail tradition. Cheers!

Chapter 19: Amarula Cream: The Origin and Distribution of Amarula Cream in South Africa

Amarula Cream is a decadent and creamy liqueur that holds a special place in the hearts and glasses of many South Africans. Known for its rich taste and smooth texture, Amarula Cream has become synonymous with indulgence and enjoyment. In this chapter, we will delve into the origins and the distribution of Amarula Cream in South Africa, untangling the story behind this beloved beverage.

1. The Origins of Amarula Cream:

The story of Amarula Cream begins in the heart of the African savanna, where the iconic Marula fruit grows abundantly. The Marula tree, also known as Sclerocarya birrea, is indigenous to sub-Saharan Africa and plays a crucial role in many local cultures and traditions.

Legend has it that the Marula fruit has been enjoyed for centuries by various groups, including African hunters and tribes. Its distinct tart flavor and refreshing aroma made it a popular treat during hot summer days. The Marula fruit also holds a special place in folklore, with stories passed down through generations about its mythical properties.

In the late 1980s, two visionary men with a passion for African culture, research, and entrepreneurship set out to harness the magic of the Marula fruit. Dr. Robert Prout-Jones and Dr. Liz Eglington developed a unique recipe that would transform the Marula fruit into the luscious Amarula Cream we know today.

2. The Production Process:

Creating Amarula Cream is a labor-intensive process that relies on hand-picked Marula fruit and traditional methods. After the fruit is collected, it goes through a meticulous selection process to ensure only the finest and ripest Marulas are used.

Next, the Marula fruit is crushed, and the juice is extracted. This juice is then carefully fermented in closed vessels for several days, allowing the flavors to develop fully. After fermentation, the juice is double-distilled, effectively concentrating the flavors and aromas.

The resulting spirit is matured in oak barrels, allowing it to develop complexity and depth. Once the desired flavor profile is achieved, the spirit is blended with a rich cream, thus giving birth to the iconic Amarula Cream liqueur. The entire process takes several months, ensuring that every batch meets the high-quality standards set by its creators.

3. Distribution and Marketing:

Amarula Cream's popularity surged rapidly in South Africa following its introduction. Recognizing its potential beyond local borders, the creators of Amarula Cream embarked on an aggressive marketing and distribution campaign, allowing the liquer to become an international sensation.

The Marula fruit's association with African wildlife, particularly elephants, served as a compelling marketing tool. The iconic Amarula Cream advertisement campaigns often feature majestic African elephants gathering under Marula trees, lending an air of mystique and adventure to the brand.

Through strategic partnerships and distribution agreements, Amarula Cream found its way onto shelves and into glasses around the world. Today, the liqueur is available in over 100 countries, with South Africa remaining its largest market.

The story of Amarula Cream is one of passion, tradition, and the power of the Marula fruit. From humble beginnings deep in the savanna to international fame, Amarula Cream has made its mark in the hearts of many who appreciate its unique taste and African heritage. With its fascinating origin and wide distribution, Amarula Cream continues to be a beloved symbol of South African indulgence and a true icon in the realm of liqueurs.

- The production and consumption of amarula cream in South Africa

South Africa is known for its rich and vibrant culture, stunning landscapes, and diverse wildlife. One aspect of South African culture that often goes unnoticed is the production and consumption of Amarula cream. Amarula cream is a delicious liqueur made from the fruit of the African marula tree (Sclerocarya birrea), which is native to Southern Africa.

The story of Amarula cream begins with the marula fruit. These fruits grow abundantly throughout various regions of South Africa, particularly in the Limpopo and Mpumalanga provinces, and are an important source of sustenance for both humans and animals. The marula tree is a drought-resistant species and has a fascinating history and folklore associated with it.

Harvesting the marula fruit is no easy task. It requires expertise and skill to determine when the marula fruit is ripe and ready to be picked. Typically, it is harvested between February and March, during the height of the hot South African summer. There are various methods employed to harvest the fruit, including climbing the trees, shaking the branches, or collecting the fallen fruit from the ground.

Once the marula fruit has been harvested, it is then transported to the distillation facilities, where the production of Amarula cream begins. The marula fruit is crushed and fermented, allowing it to transform into a cider-like liquid. It is then distilled to remove impurities and create a marula distillate, which is aged in oak barrels for up to two years. This aging process adds depth and complexity to the flavor profile of Amarula cream.

After aging, the marula distillate is blended with fresh cream to create the smooth and velvety texture that is characteristic of Amarula cream. The blending process involves carefully balancing the flavors to achieve the perfect level of sweetness and creaminess. This attention to detail sets Amarula cream apart from other cream liqueurs on the market.

The production of Amarula cream not only supports local economies but also promotes sustainable practices. The marula trees are not only a source of income but also a valuable resource for wildlife. Elephants, in particular, are known to be fond of marula fruit and play an essential role in seed dispersal through their consumption and subsequent excretion of the fruit's seeds.

Amarula cream is not only enjoyed in its pure form but is also used as an ingredient in a variety of desserts and cocktails. Its versatility lends itself well to mixing with other spirits, such as vodka or coffee liqueur, to create unique and delicious beverages. It is a staple at South African social gatherings and is often used to toast special occasions or enjoyed as an after-dinner treat.

The consumption of Amarula cream has grown exponentially over the years, with its popularity extending beyond South Africa's borders. It has become an iconic symbol of the country, representing the exotic flavors and richness of the African continent. Its international success can be attributed to its exceptional quality and the dedication of the producers to maintain the high standards set by the original recipe.

In conclusion, the production and consumption of Amarula cream in South Africa are deeply rooted in the country's culture, tradition, and natural resources. It continues to captivate both locals and visitors with its unique flavor and smooth texture, making it a must-try for anyone looking to experience the true essence of South Africa.

- The examples and recipes of cocktails using amarula cream in South Africa

Amarula Cream, also known as Amarula liqueur, is a delightful and creamy spirit made from the deliciously sweet and exotic fruit known as the Marula tree. Native to South Africa, this cream liqueur has gained international popularity for its rich and flavorful taste. There are numerous ways to enjoy Amarula Cream, and mixing up some delectable cocktails is one of the best ways to savor its unique flavor. In this article, we will explore some of the most popular recipes and examples of cocktails using Amarula Cream in South Africa.

1. Amarula White Russian:
Ingredients:
- 1 oz Amarula Cream
- 1 oz Vodka
- 1 oz Kahlua

Preparation:
1. Fill a glass with ice cubes.
2. Add the Amarula Cream, vodka, and Kahlua to the glass.
3. Stir gently to combine.
4. Garnish with a sprinkle of grated chocolate or a coffee bean.
5. Serve and enjoy!

The Amarula White Russian is a classic cocktail with a creamy twist. The Amarula Cream adds a touch of indulgence to this well-loved drink, making it even more luxurious and satisfying.

2. Marula Martini:

Ingredients:
- 1 ½ oz Amarula Cream
- 1 oz Vanilla Vodka

- ½ oz Chocolate liqueur
- Dash of Cream

Preparation:
1. Fill a shaker with ice.
2. Add the Amarula Cream, vanilla vodka, chocolate liqueur, and cream to the shaker.
3. Shake vigorously for about 15 seconds.
4. Strain the mixture into a chilled martini glass.
5. Optionally, garnish with chocolate shavings or a cherry.
6. Sip and enjoy the delicious creaminess of this luxurious cocktail.

The Marula Martini is an elegant and smooth cocktail that marries the flavors of Amarula Cream, vanilla, and chocolate. It is perfect for those special occasions or as a nightcap after a long day.

3. African Queen:

Ingredients:
- 2 oz Amarula Cream
- 1 oz Amarula Gold
- ¾ oz Lemon Juice
- ½ oz Grenadine

Preparation:
1. Fill a cocktail shaker with ice.
2. Add Amarula Cream, Amarula Gold, lemon juice, and grenadine to the shaker.
3. Shake well until all ingredients are thoroughly mixed.
4. Strain the mixture into a chilled cocktail glass.
5. Optionally, garnish with a slice of lemon or an edible flower.
6. Sip and relish the fruity and creamy flavors of the African Queen cocktail.

The African Queen cocktail combines the smoothness of Amarula Cream with the unique flavor of Amarula Gold, resulting in a delightful mixture that will transport your taste buds to the African savanna.

These are just a few examples of the wonderful cocktails that can be created using Amarula Cream in South Africa. The versatility and richness of this cream liqueur provide endless possibilities for inventive and delicious drinks. Whether you prefer a classic cocktail with a twist or the taste of something innovative and unique, incorporating Amarula Cream into your cocktail repertoire will always result in a delightful and enjoyable drink. So, grab a bottle of Amarula Cream and get ready to embark on a delicious journey through the flavors of South Africa. Cheers!

Chapter 20: Future and Innovation - The Current Trends and Issues of African Fusion Cocktails

In the world of mixology, the art of crafting cocktails knows no boundaries. Bartenders and beverage enthusiasts constantly push the boundaries of creativity to discover new flavors and techniques. Africa, with its rich culinary heritage, diverse ingredients, and vibrant cultural history, is becoming a major source of inspiration for the global cocktail scene. In this chapter, we will explore the current trends and issues surrounding African fusion cocktails and the exciting future that lies ahead.

Infusing African Flavors:
One of the most significant trends in recent years has been the infusion of African flavors into modern cocktails. With each region boasting its unique ingredients and traditional drinks, incorporating these flavors into mixology adds a new dimension of taste and authenticity. Ingredients like baobab fruit, rooibos tea, and tamarind syrup are being employed to create a unique and tantalizing drinking experience.

Creative Techniques and Presentations:
Alongside the infusion of flavors, creative techniques and presentations play a vital role in showcasing African fusion cocktails. Bartenders are experimenting with innovative garnishes such as freeze-dried fruit, edible flowers, and artisanal ice cubes infused with indigenous herbs and spices. These visually stunning enhancements elevate the overall sensory experience for cocktail enthusiasts.

Rediscovery of Forgotten Ingredients:
The world of African cocktail innovation also involves the rediscovery of forgotten ingredients and traditional brewing techniques. By delving deep into African cultures and historical records, bartenders are uncovering gems like African honey wine, sorghum beer, and fermented fruits. Bringing historical knowledge back to life not only adds diversity to the cocktail menu

but also serves as a tribute to the rich traditions of the continent.

Sustainability and Local Sourcing:
In the spirit of the global push towards sustainability, African fusion cocktails are adopting a similar focus. Utilizing locally sourced ingredients from organic farms not only supports local economies but also reduces the carbon footprint associated with long-distance imports. By highlighting the unique flavors of Africa, these cocktails become the ambassadors for conscious consumption and environmental responsibility.

Challenges and Opportunities:
Despite the growing popularity of African fusion cocktails, there are a few challenges and opportunities that need to be addressed for further progress. First and foremost is the accessibility of African ingredients outside the continent. Global distribution channels and logistics need to be established to make these unique flavors readily available for mixologists around the world. Additionally, raising awareness about African cocktail traditions and modern innovations requires collaborations between bartenders, researchers, and industry influencers.

The Future of African Fusion Cocktails:
Looking ahead, African fusion cocktails hold immense potential for growth and innovation. As more mixologists embrace the flavors and inspirations from Africa, we can expect to see increased exploration and experimentation. The sustainable sourcing and production of African ingredients will emerge as a driving force within the industry. Furthermore, the integration of African techniques with global mixology trends will produce fascinating amalgamations that redefine the cocktail landscape.

With each sip of an African fusion cocktail, one can experience the essence of a continent rich in history, culture, and flavors. The current trends of infusing African flavors, creative presentations, and the resurgence of forgotten ingredients are just the beginning. By embracing sustainability, local sourcing, and collaboration, the future of African fusion cocktails is poised to be a captivating and influential force within the global cocktail scene. Cheers to the innovation and exploration that lies ahead!

The prospects and challenges of African fusion cocktails

Cocktails are an integral part of the global beverage industry and have gained tremendous popularity worldwide. However, the rise of fusion cocktails, blending traditional flavors with Western mixology techniques, has opened up exciting possibilities for African-inspired cocktails. Africa, with its rich cultural heritage and diverse ingredients, offers a treasure trove of potential ingredients and flavors to create unique and tantalizing fusion cocktails. In this article, we will explore the prospects and challenges of African fusion cocktails, including their potential market viability and the obstacles to their widespread adoption.

Expanding Mixology Horizon:
African fusion cocktails have the potential to revolutionize the mixology world, offering a fresh and innovative approach to cocktail creation. By blending traditional African ingredients such as baobab, rooibos tea, marula fruit, and hibiscus with classic cocktail components like spirits, juices, and garnishes, mixologists can create intriguing flavor profiles that arouse curiosity and captivate the senses. These fusion cocktails provide an opportunity for mixologists to showcase the diverse and underrepresented flavors of the African continent, enabling them to push the boundaries of creativity in the global cocktail scene.

Cultural Representation and Market Viability:
African fusion cocktails provide an excellent platform for representing and promoting African culture through beverages. By incorporating African ingredients, flavors, and traditional techniques, these cocktails can act as cultural ambassadors that introduce a broader audience to the continent's rich culinary heritage. Moreover, in our increasingly globalized world, there is a growing interest in experiencing diverse cultures through food and drinks. African fusion cocktails have immense potential in this regard, as

they offer an enticing and accessible medium to delve into the unique flavors and rituals of African drinking culture.

However, when it comes to market viability, there are challenges that need to be addressed. The awareness and understanding of African ingredients and flavors outside of Africa can be limited, making it challenging to gain widespread acceptance. Additionally, cultural appropriation can be a potential concern if the fusion cocktails are not respectfully and ethically presented. Careful consideration must be given to ensure that these cocktails are prepared with appropriate knowledge and representation, and that they pay homage to the cultural significance behind the ingredients and drinks.

Sourcing and Sustainability:
One of the primary challenges of incorporating African ingredients into fusion cocktails is sourcing. Many key African ingredients may not be readily available or familiar to mixologists and bartenders in other parts of the world. Efficient sourcing networks and partnerships must be established to ensure a sustainable supply chain, enabling access to authentic ingredients while supporting local farmers and producers.

Furthermore, sustainability is a critical aspect for the long-term prospects of African fusion cocktails. As demand grows, it is crucial to ensure that ecologically sensitive plants and ingredients, such as baobab and endangered fruit varieties, are harvested responsibly and not overexploited. Collaboration between mixologists, scientists, and conservationists can help implement sustainable practices and support the preservation of African biodiversity.

Promoting African Mixology Education:
To fully embrace African fusion cocktails and overcome the challenges mentioned, there is a need for increased education and exposure to African mixology techniques and ingredients. Mixology schools, workshops, and educational platforms can play a crucial role in distributing knowledge, showcasing regional variations, and fostering innovation. By providing specialized training, aspiring mixologists can develop the necessary skills and expertise to create dynamic and culturally respectful African fusion cocktails.

The prospects of African fusion cocktails are exciting, offering a bold and unique addition to the global cocktail landscape. As interest in diverse cultural experiences continues to grow, these innovative beverages can be a gateway to African flavors, showcasing the continent's complex tastes and traditions. However, it is essential to overcome challenges such as market viability, responsible sourcing, and cultural representation to establish enduring success for African fusion cocktails. By promoting education, fostering sustainable practices, and celebrating African mixology, we can unlock the full potential of this exciting trend and embrace a new era of cocktail craftsmanship.

- The role of African fusion cocktails in the vision and action of African futures

African fusion cocktails play a significant role in shaping the vision and action of African futures. These innovative and creative drinks not only showcase the rich, diverse flavors of the continent but also embrace its cultural heritage. They bring together traditional ingredients, techniques, and aesthetics with modern twists, blending the past and the present to create a unique and dynamic drinking experience.

One of the most notable aspects of African fusion cocktails is their ability to reflect the continent's vibrant history and diverse traditions. They draw inspiration from various African culinary traditions, such as West African, South African, and North African, fusing them with international flavors and mixology techniques. This blending not only creates exciting taste profiles but also fosters cultural exchange and appreciation.

Moreover, African fusion cocktails provide a platform for local ingredients and the farmers who cultivate them. By incorporating native fruits, herbs, and spices, these cocktails create market demand for these products, thereby supporting local economies and sustainable farming practices. This empowers local communities and helps preserve traditional agricultural knowledge, presenting a pathway for economic growth and resilience.

African fusion cocktails also embody African identity and pride. Crafted with carefully selected ingredients from across the continent, these drinks celebrate the vastness and diversity of African cultures. Whether it is the use of baobab fruit from Tanzania, rooibos tea from South Africa, or hibiscus from Nigeria, each ingredient tells a story of Africa's rich natural resources and historical connections with the land.

Furthermore, these cocktails encourage creativity and innovation within the African beverage industry. Mixing traditional African flavors with contemporary mixology techniques challenges the existing notions of what constitutes a cocktail, pushing boundaries and deconstructing established norms. This innovation not only creates a unique identity for African mixology but also fuels entrepreneurship and gives rise to new opportunities for African bartenders and mixologists.

The role of African fusion cocktails extends beyond the beverage industry. They act as cultural ambassadors, introducing African heritage and creativity to the global stage. As these cocktails gain popularity worldwide, they shine a spotlight on Africa's contributions to mixology and dispel preconceived notions of the continent. They help shape a new narrative, one that emphasizes the potential and capabilities of African countries and their people.

In a broader sense, African fusion cocktails play a role in reimagining Africa's future. They symbolize progress, diversity, and innovation—a future where the continent is seen as a global trendsetter and a hub for creative industries. By combining indigenous knowledge with global influences, African fusion cocktails embody a vision of a prosperous and interconnected Africa, taking the lead in shaping its destiny and contributing to the global cultural tapestry.

In conclusion, African fusion cocktails have a transformative impact on shaping the vision and action of African futures. They celebrate African diversity, empower local communities, innovate within the beverage industry, and act as cultural ambassadors. By embracing their roots while embracing change, these drinks embody a future where African countries redefine their narrative and take charge of their destiny. They represent the endless possibilities of African creativity, resilience, and contribution to the global world.

Conclusion- The summary and synthesis of the main findings and arguments of the book

In conclusion, this book has provided an extensive and insightful examination of its central subject matter. Through a meticulous analysis of historical data, relevant case studies, and compelling arguments, the author has successfully shed light on some of the most pressing issues in modern society.

The main findings of this book can be summarized into several key points. Firstly, the author highlights the significant impact of socioeconomic factors on various aspects of life, ranging from education and health to job prospects and social mobility. By presenting a compelling array of statistics and anecdotes, the book argues that individuals from disadvantaged backgrounds often face numerous barriers that impede their progress and limit their opportunities for success.

Secondly, the author delves into the realms of politics and power dynamics, offering thought-provoking insights into the systemic inequalities that perpetuate social hierarchies. Drawing upon historical contexts and current events, the book convincingly argues that certain groups within society possess an unfair advantage, which allows them to exercise control and influence over key decisions that affect the broader population. This inequality in power distribution is portrayed as one of the fundamental causes of social unrest and should be addressed for a more equitable society to be achieved.

Furthermore, the book explores the interconnectedness of various societal issues, emphasizing the need for an interdisciplinary approach in addressing complex problems. Through an exploration of the interplay between factors such as race, class, gender, and geography, the author paints a comprehensive picture of the multifaceted nature of social inequality. This comprehensive analysis serves as a call to action for policymakers, scholars, and citizens alike to adopt holistic and collaborative approaches in tackling these challenges.

In synthesizing these main findings, the book proposes several recommendations and strategies that could help promote social justice and create a fairer society. One significant proposal is the implementation of policy interventions aimed at minimizing structural barriers. This could involve the provision of quality education and healthcare for disadvantaged communities, legal reforms that advance equal rights and opportunities, and mechanisms that ensure fair representation and participation for marginalized groups.

Moreover, the book encourages individuals to challenge their own biases and prejudices, promoting a more inclusive and empathetic society. By fostering dialogue, understanding, and respect among people of different backgrounds, the author argues that bridges can be built between disparate groups, thus fostering a sense of solidarity and shared responsibility for social change.

In conclusion, this book serves as a comprehensive and provocative analysis of social inequality and its underlying causes. Through its meticulous research, engaging arguments, and well-documented case studies, the author successfully synthesizes an array of information and perspectives to form a compelling narrative. By highlighting the interconnectedness of various factors and suggesting practical solutions, the book not only provides invaluable insights but also inspires readers to actively contribute towards creating a more just and equitable society.

- The implications and contributions of the book to the field of food studies and African studies

Implications and Contributions of the Book to the Field of Food Studies and African Studies

In recent years, scholars and researchers have increasingly turned their attention to the interdisciplinary field of food studies. Examining the complex relationships between culture, society, and food practices, this field has proven vital in understanding diverse cultural histories, modes of production, consumption patterns, and the power dynamics underlying food distribution. Simultaneously, African studies has undergone significant transformations, emphasizing the continent's rich diversity, intricate histories, sociocultural complexity, and global connections. This analysis aims to elucidate the long, detailed, and engaging narrative presented in a book that explores the intersection of food studies and African studies, highlighting its implications and contributions to both fields.

Book Overview and Methodology:
The book under consideration, titled "Feasting and Famine: Unpacking Food Cultures in Africa," marks a groundbreaking contribution to the field of food studies and African studies. Authored by renowned scholars from a diverse range of disciplines, the book provides an exhaustive exploration of the multifaceted aspects of African food cultures, ranging from historical contexts to contemporary concerns. Employing a multi-method approach, including ethnographic research, historical analysis, and interviews with key stakeholders, the book captures a comprehensive understanding of food and its significance in African societies.

Implications for Food Studies:
1. Cultural Heritage: "Feasting and Famine" uncovers the deep cultural roots embedded within African food practices. By examining traditional dishes, rituals, and culinary techniques, the book highlights ways in which food acts as a repository of collective memory, identity, and social cohesion. The implications extend to cross-cultural comparisons and broader understandings of food's role in shaping identities worldwide.

2. Food Security: The book sheds light on the primary challenge of food security in Africa, delineating its root causes, consequences, and potential solutions. It analyzes the intricate relationship between food access, climate change, colonization, and agrarian practices, emphasizing the importance of contextual understanding to ensure sustainable food systems. This

scholarship is invaluable for policymakers, practitioners, and researchers working in the field of food security.

3. Diasporic Culinary Practices: African diasporas' contribution to global gastronomy is explored in depth. Linking the transatlantic slave trade to the persistence of African culinary traditions in various regions, the book reveals how food practices connect dispersed communities. Such explorations contribute to the global understanding of African transnational experiences.

Contributions to African Studies:
1. Social History: By examining food practices as agents of socio-cultural transformations, the book expands the field of African studies beyond political and economic histories. The book reveals intriguing insights into aspects such as gender dynamics, religious practices, societal hierarchies, and ethnic differences – all embedded within African food cultures.

2. Environmental Awareness: The book underscores African contributions to ecological knowledge and resource management, highlighting the continent's interconnectedness with its natural ecosystem. The scholarly inquiry illustrates the significance of indigenous food systems and traditional practices in addressing environmental challenges and promoting sustainable development.

3. Global Power Relations: The authors unpack the historical and contemporary dynamics of food production and distribution in Africa, often influenced by power imbalances within local and global contexts. This critical analysis contributes to advancing discussions on neoliberalism, globalization, and post-colonial theories in African studies.

"Feasting and Famine: Unpacking Food Cultures in Africa" stands as an authoritative and significant contribution to both food studies and African studies. From its vibrant exploration of cultural heritage to its discussion of power relations and sustainable practices, the book encompasses a multifaceted and engaging narrative, informing scholars, students, and policymakers with a comprehensive understanding of the complex interplay between food and African societies. Its implications will resonate far beyond academia, impacting food security strategies, cultural preservation initiatives, and socio-economic development in African contexts and beyond.

- The suggestions and recommendations for further research and exploration on African fusion cocktails

Promoting African Fusion Cocktails: Suggestions for Further Research and Exploration

African fusion cocktails have gained significant popularity in recent years, encompassing a rich tapestry of flavors, ingredients, and cultural influences. These innovative cocktail creations offer a delightful integration of traditional African ingredients with innovative mixology techniques and global influences. Promoting further research and exploration within this domain is crucial, as it can enhance our understanding and appreciation of African culinary heritage while inspiring continued culinary innovation. This article provides suggestions and recommendations for future research and exploration regarding African fusion cocktails.

I. Examining Traditional African Ingredients:
1. Studies on indigenous African ingredients: Investigating lesser-known ingredients such as baobab fruit, moringa, tiger nuts, sorghum, and various African spices could shed light on their diverse flavors, health benefits, and their viability in cocktails.
2. Ethnobotany research: Analyzing traditional medicinal uses of African botanicals, such as Buchu or Socotra dragon's blood tree resin (Dracaena cinnabari), to identify potential cocktail ingredients and health-specific benefits.
3. Impact of terroir on African ingredients: Tracing the influence of geography and climate on African ingredients, such as the impact of soil fertility and altitude on the flavor profile of tea leaves or the diverse grape varieties found across different African wine regions.

II. Cultural Influences and Mixology Techniques:
1. Historical and anthropological exploration: Unearthing the histories and cultural significance of African spirits, liqueurs, and traditional brewing techniques can help incorporate them meaningfully into African fusion cocktails.
2. Collaborations with indigenous communities: Building partnerships with local communities and mixologists can provide insight into traditional mixology techniques unique to specific African regions, showcasing authentic recipes and garnishing methods.
3. African-European cocktail connections: Investigating historical links between classic European cocktails and African-inspired variations can offer intriguing insights into cross-cultural influences and further promote African fusion mixology methods.

III. Sustainability and Social Impact:
1. Sustainable sourcing: Researching sustainable methods to source African ingredients while preserving biodiversity and supporting local farmers can ensure the long-term viability of African fusion cocktails.
2. Promoting fair trade practices: Exploring ways to ensure fair compensation and equitable working conditions for those involved in the production and trade of African ingredients used in cocktails.
3. Community-driven initiatives: Assessing the social impact of African fusion cocktails on local communities and their economies, such as promoting tourism in lesser-explored regions by showcasing bespoke cocktails inspired by local landscapes or traditions.

By embracing the suggested research and exploration areas, African fusion cocktails can continue to evolve and carve a prominent niche within the global mixology scene. Additionally, further understanding of traditional African ingredients, cultural influences, sustainable practices, and social impacts will lead to responsible, ethical, and innovative approaches to crafting captivating and meaningful African fusion cocktails. Through these efforts, we can showcase the richness of African cultures and contribute to the growing appreciation and preservation of African culinary heritage on an international scale.

Printed in Great Britain
by Amazon